WEST SUSSEX INNS

Other Sussex Titles by Countryside Books

THE EAST SUSSEX VILLAGE BOOK
Rupert Taylor

THE WEST SUSSEX VILLAGE BOOK
Tony Wales

SUSSEX SCANDALS
Rupert Taylor

TALES OF OLD SUSSEX
Lillian Candlin

A SUSSEX GARLAND
Tony Wales

SUSSEX RAILWAYS REMEMBERED
Leslie Oppitz

SUSSEX SHIPWRECKS
Nicholas Thornton

GHOSTS OF SUSSEX
Judy Middleton

EAST SUSSEX INNS
Brigid Chapman

For a complete catalogue of Countryside Books' titles please write to:

The Publicity Manager
Countryside Books
3 Catherine Road
Newbury
Berkshire
RG14 7NA

WEST SUSSEX INNS

Brigid Chapman

With Illustrations by the author

COUNTRYSIDE BOOKS
NEWBURY, BERKSHIRE

First Published 1988

COUNTRYSIDE BOOKS
3 Catherine Road
Newbury, Berkshire

ISBN 1 85306 023 2

Cover illustration by John Baker

Produced through MRM Associates, Reading
Typeset by J&L Composition Ltd, Filey, North Yorkshire
Printed in England by J.W. Arrowsmith Ltd., Bristol

To Terry, with love

ACKNOWLEDGEMENTS

So many people have contributed fascinating facts about the history of the inns of West Sussex: Keith and Janet Smith of Mill Press, East Wittering; Peter Ogden, chairman of Selsey Parish Council; Mr Eric Holden of Penlands Vale, Steyning; Mrs Deirdre Light of Kingsfold; members of the Local History Societies of Hurstpierpoint and Petworth.

Historian and licensee of the Murrell Arms, Barnham, Mr Mervyn Cutten, was kind enough to let me browse through his files of facts on the inns of Sussex and Mr P. J. Bariff, company surveyor, and Mr David Mallard, Tied Trade manager of King and Barnes Ltd, 18 Bishopric, Horsham, provided some vital information about their brewery's houses.

And the licensees of the inns of West Sussex did their best to find the answers to questions of history . . . as did their customers who went to great lengths to help with my research. Thank you all so much.

Brigid Chapman
1988

INTRODUCTION

THINGS have been happening in the pubs of West Sussex since the Romans played dice for dinarii beneath the streets of Chichester, which they called Noviomagus or Regnum. A pair of the dice they used are preserved behind glass in the wall of the Old Cross Inn in North Street, their discovery confirming the theory that the cellar of the inn was once a Roman gambling den.

When the legions were recalled to defend Rome in AD 410 new invaders swept in from North Germany and the Baltic seaboard. By AD 447 the whole of Sussex and Surrey was under the rule of Ella, King of the South Saxons. The Anglo-Saxons were great ones for their ale – so great in fact that some controls over their drinking had to be introduced. In the reign of King Edgar (AD 957–975) the number of ale houses – from the Old English word aleu-hus – had to be restricted to one per village.

Drinking was a communal activity and large, wooden tankards would be passed from hand to hand. The ale in them was measured by wooden pegs placed at half pint intervals – hence the expressions 'have a peg' and 'take him down a peg'.

With the spread of Christianity throughout Southern England came the need for more elaborate places for rest and refreshment than the occasional alehouse. Pilgrims were constantly on the move from one shrine to another and the monks did what they could to encourage this perambulating source of revenue. Hospices were set up along the favoured routes and travellers would be provided with accommodation according to their rank. The top people who merited the top rooms would have to pay the top prices for fine wines from France, venison from the abbot's woods and carp from his fishponds. The less wealthy and well-connected would get ale brewed by the monks – then the best brewers in Europe – plenty of plain food and a dry bed for the night.

The church was quick to appreciate the money-making potential of a good brew. Church ales, the precursors of the coffee morning and garden fête, were introduced to raise funds for necessary repairs. The parishioners would provide the barley and the churchwardens would brew strong ale from it and sell it for consumption on the church premises – inside in the winter, or if wet, and in the churchyard on fine summer days. Things frequently got a bit out of hand on these occasions and St Dunstan, when he was Archbishop of Canterbury, issued a number of edicts against intemperance at church ales.

What the church had started the laity continued and soon there were all sorts of ales – bride ales, wedding ales, midsummer ales. Bottle parties had begun.

It was the Puritans who put a stop to the general jollity. Before the Civil War, when the population of England and Wales was about 3¾ million, there were 14,202 alehouses, 1,631 inns and 329 taverns. The average consumption of ale and beer was about two quarts per head per day but then what alternative was there? In towns particularly it was safer to drink ale than water because methods of sewage control were primitive. The contents of chamber pots were poured from upstairs windows to the streets below and washed from there into the rivers and wells, whenever it rained.

Under the Commonwealth, innkeepers were faced with all sorts of rules and regulations. It became an offence to hold any sort of ale, or to dance round the maypole. Horse racing was banned, theatres were closed and church-going enforced. This dismal state of affairs lasted for 11 years and it took the inns of England another 150 years – to the heyday of the coaching era – really to recover from it.

Not all of them did recover because Charles II accepted the tax on beer as part of his annual income of £120,000. In 1689 it was raised from 2s to 3s 3d a barrel and then leapt to 6s 6d a barrel at the outbreak of war with France. Another blow to the English inn was the Act permitting the distillation of spirits from home grown corn. Its object was to restrict imports of French brandy and to increase the consumption of home grown cereals but it was disastrous to the health of the nation.

Everyone started to distil their own gin, or genever, a colourless spirit brought over from the Low Countries by William of Orange, and soon there were hundreds of back street bars advertising 'drunk for a penny, dead drunk for twopence, and the straw is free. ...'

In 1734, 6 million gallons of distilled spirits were consumed by 6 million people – and among the 6 million were little children. In 1736 there was enough gin about to stock 9,000 shops in London alone and between 1740 and 1742, in the London area, there were twice as many burials as baptisms.

Gradually it dawned on Church and State that something would have to be done to stop people drinking themselves to death. Stricter licensing laws, tea and the temperance movement gradually brought the gin era to an end. By 1760 the annual consumption of spirits had dropped to 2 million gallons. 'The people themselves seem at length to have discovered that health and pleasure, food and raiment, are better than sickness and pain, want and wretchedness' wrote Jonas Hanway, known not only for his good works among the poor but for popularising the use of the umbrella.

It was tea, together with coffee and chocolate, which did as much if not more than temperance to stop Britain's long binge. These non-alcoholic beverages had come into the country from 1650 onwards but they were expensive. Tea at £3 a pound, was beyond the reach of men hard put to earn that amount in a year.

But as 18th century merchant adventurers opened up new trade routes tea and other beverages, together with scents, silks and spices, poured into the country. Soon the cups that cheer but not inebriate were at everyone's lips – and the boiling water used to make their contents killed off a lot of bacteria and so helped the health of the nation.

Tea drinking did not do the inns of Sussex a great deal of good but they benefited from the need to smuggle it into the country to avoid the heavy duty on imports imposed by Parliament. Smuggling gangs selected certain inns to be their headquarters. An arrangement would be made with the innkeeper, places of concealment for the contraband devised, meetings held, operations planned and smuggled goods shared out in comfort and safety.

To begin with the smugglers were treated as friends by the rural communities they served and many a parson got his brandy from them, many a parish clerk his tobacco. But as law enforcement became more rigorous and the smugglers more greedy, there were some horrific instances of violence and brutality. One of the nastiest murders took place in the Dog and Partridge at Slindon – and it was all for nothing.

A young man, Richard Hawkins, was thought to have stolen some tea from a cache of contraband. He was lured to the inn – only a wall of which now remains – where he was stripped naked and beaten with whips. When he drew up his knees to protect his stomach he was whipped on the genitals. So great was the pain that he screamed out that his father and brother had taken the tea.

Having extracted this confession his attackers propped him in a chair by the parlour fire and went back to their drinks to discuss what to do next. After a glass or two they noticed that the young man by the fire was dead. They left him where he was and went off to report to their leaders. 'Get rid of the body' they were told so they returned to the inn with the intention of dropping the remains of Richard Hawkins down the nearest well and putting it about that he had taken ship for France. But to this the innkeeper, James Reynolds, objected. The nearest well was in his garden and he had carefully kept out of the way during the murder and wanted no connection with the corpse. After an argument the murderers rode 10 miles across country to Parham Park where they dumped the body, weighted with stones, into a lake. Next day they checked their stock of tea again. They had made a mistake, there was none missing.

The murder of Richard Hawkins took place on 28th January 1748. Exactly a year later one of his murderers, John Miles, son of Richard Miles of the Hawkhurst gang, was hanged in chains from a gibbet near the Dog and Partridge. His accomplice, Jeremiah Curtis, escaped to France and the innkeeper, Reynolds, was acquitted on a charge of accessory to murder. He produced several neighbours who swore that he was with them at the time.

Smugglers brought some prosperity and a certain amount of notoriety to the inns of Sussex but it was the improvement in communications that provided a real boost to business. In the last half of the 18th century 1,600 Road Acts were passed – a road building boom had begun and the coaches started to roll.

Old taverns were spruced up and new inns were built to cater for the increased demand for rest and refreshment, and for somewhere to change the horses. The new buildings were nearly all of the same pattern with plain stone fronts, simple sash windows and an arched access to an inner courtyard and stables. These archways were not always wide enough to cope with coaches carrying outside passengers. One sorry incident is related by Charles Dickens in *The Pickwick Papers.* Mr Jingle is speaking: 'Other day – five children, mother – tall lady, eating sandwiches – forgot the arch – crash – knock – children look round – mother's head off, sandwich in her hand – no mouth to put it in – head of family off – shocking! shocking!'

The mail coaches, introduced in 1784, cut hours off inter-city travel. Horses were changed frequently and so quickly that any passenger alighting to go to the privy or for some other purpose was likely to find, unless he was particularly quick about it, that his luggage and the coach had gone.

For about 80 years the owners of the inns on the main coaching routes never had it so good. There would be passengers arriving at all hours – perhaps the Prince of Wales and his entourage one minute, coming via Cuckfield to his pretty pavilion in Brighton – and then a common coachload of commercial travellers. These 'common coaches' were not noted for their comfort and their passengers did not get much of a welcome from the innkeepers according to a report in the *Sussex Advertiser* in 1791. 'By common stage you are classed with company of every description', it states. 'You are also paid no attention to at the inns where you stop, although you pay exorbitant for refreshment'.

That situation was soon to change. Warning puffs of smoke on the horizon heralded the coming of the railways and there were no longer coachloads of customers clattering into the courtyards. Many of the large coaching inns closed for good and were turned into private houses. The smaller ones kept going with local trade and by selling out to the nearest brewery and selling only its beer.

The railways not only removed the traffic from the roads – they also brought people from the country into the towns where there was plenty of work in the new industries and at higher wages. This immigration helped the town pub but harmed the village inns. Town pubs became true 'public houses', a term first used in 1854 by a House of Commons Select Committee. They were centres for all kinds of community activity. Inquests were held in them, town councils dined in them, magistrates met in them, friendly societies were formed in them, they were the scene of soirees, concerts and assemblies of all kinds and political parties used them as their headquarters. In Chichester, for instance, no Whig would step across the threshold of the Tory Dolphin, nor a single Tory enter the Whig Anchor. Today such niceties of political choice cannot be exercised, the Dolphin and Anchor is one hotel.

Hardly had the licensed trade adjusted to the railways and was looking hopefully towards the cyclists, the motorcyclists and the drivers of the new motor cars, when there was yet another war.

This time it was not just a question of taxing beer to pay for the conflict – the government was determined to stop people drinking so that they could concentrate on war work. In 1915 Lloyd George introduced the Defence of the Realm Act (DORA) and for the first time pub opening hours were restricted by law. In the areas where it was considered essential for the war effort they were not allowed to open before noon and had to close at 2.30pm for the afternoon. Six years later a Licensing Act was introduced confirming these restrictions and extending them to nearly all licensed premises.

It was even worse in the Second World War. Many pubs were bombed, blasted or burned out of existence and the ones that remained open found supplies difficult to get. Everything went under the counter except the customers who could not get enough to drink to put them there.

The past 40 years or so of comparative peace have seen even more changes in the licensed trade. Today, to counteract the effect of the breathalyser and the easy availability of drink from supermarket shelves, the accent is on food. Gone are the days of a pint and a peanut by the porch. Most inns offer lavish bar snacks or full meals at lunchtime and in the evening. Many even have a restaurant as part of the pub. And there is a tendency towards entertainment. Some provide live music at weekends or have regular Folk or Country and Western evenings, others want to attract the whole family and offer special facilities for children. The Red Lion at Ashington has books in its bars for customers to have a quiet read.

The biggest change of all is towards benevolence. As the ensuing pages show, what has happened in the past in the pubs of West Sussex has been fairly horrific. There are many cases of murder and mayhem, greed and ghastliness. Cruel sports have been practised, cruel wagers have been made. Here and there has been some humour – of the cow falling off the cliff kind – but any touches of kindness and good nature have come more from the landlords than their customers. Today it is totally different. Historians in the 21st century will be writing about the caring spirit of the 1980s, for there are not many pubs without a pile of pennies for the blind, darts marathons for the disabled, sponsored sports for the suffering.

Luke 10, 33–35 tells the story of the man who fell among thieves on the road from Jerusalem to Jericho. 'A certain Samaritan as he journeyed came where he was; and when he saw him he had compassion on him. And he went to him and bound up his wounds, pouring in oil and wine, and set him on his own beast, and brought him to an inn, and took care of him.

'And on the morrow, when he departed, he took out two pence and gave these to the host, and said unto him: Take care of him, and whatsoever thou spendest more, when I come again, I will repay thee.'

And the landlord no doubt put the extra on the slate – as landlords will do for their regulars to this day.

The Crown & Anchor, Shoreham

ADVERSANE

BLACKSMITH'S ARMS: This inn was first licensed in 1802 when it was an extension to the forge and a convenient place for farmers, grooms and travelling horsemen to drink and chat while their horses were being shod. In those days most inns brewed their own beer so it was convenient for the owner of the Arms to have a malthouse nearby to supply the basic ingredients. It was one of a number throughout Sussex owned by the Allen brothers, Alfred and Dennett, who amassed a tidy fortune by defrauding the revenue of the excise duty due on the malt they sold.

For six years from 1919 a famous son of Sussex worked at the forge and drank at the inn. He was Gauis Carley who, after 60 years as a blacksmith wrote his memoirs very much in his own words. His account of Victorian village life as it was lived was given to the West Sussex Records Office at Chichester and in 1964 the *Memories of Gauis Carley, a Sussex Blacksmith*, was published by Moore and Tillyer of Chichester for the Marc Fitch Fund. In this book Gauis Carley refers to the Blacksmith's Arms as a very old inn 'Many travellers have slept in its old oak timbered rooms' he says, but gives no further details.

Albourne

KINGS HEAD: Before this large pub with its weathered copper cupolas was built in 1934 the site was occupied – or rather the present car park was – by an old cottage alehouse with a well in the back garden. Travellers used to stop there for rest and refreshment – and get some water for their horses from the well.

After the 1896 Emancipation Run, when the private motorist got rid of the red flag and celebrated the fact with a drive to Brighton, a new class of customer called at the Kings Head. Be-goggled, leather-coated automobilists would draw off their gauntlets and reach for their drinks. They were quite likely to ask the landlord for water for the radiator of their horseless carriage and would be directed to the well to help themselves.

Since the 1930s, and particularly since the last war, the first Sunday in November sees almost the entire length of the A23 lined with spectators for the Veteran Car Run. A favourite observation point is the Kings Head car park as the cars have a fairly stiff hill to climb just before it. This is also a favourite pulling up point for any steam car on the run needing to have its boiler topped up with water – now available from the tap rather than the well in the garden.

The pub, because of its historic transport connections, became the headquarters of a club specialising in classic American cars and a group of vintage motorcycle buffs also meets there.

A bit of a shock for passing motorists is the new inn sign. The old one, which showed a man with a crown on his head, was badly damaged in the October 1987 storm and could not be repaired. Licensee Joyce Hurst did not want another indeterminate royal head so she chose another king – King Kong. He too dates, as the pub does, from the 1930s.

AMBERLEY

In 1874 there were 2,355 licensed houses in the county – one for every 176 people. Amberley had five and a population of 687 in the 1871 census, giving it one pub for every 137 people.

BLACK HORSE: Here, in December 1865, Mr B T Davis, an agent for the Friend in Need Insurance Company, delivered a lecture on the need for insurance and reminded his audience that a friendly society had once existed for this purpose in the village. However, it had been forced to close in 1862 'for sharing out what should have been kept in'. His words did not go unheeded for in January 1867, after a lecture by the Grand Master of the Manchester Oddfellows Society to '60 gentlemen and working men' the St Michael's Lodge, Amberley was formed.

Another meeting held at the Black Horse was the first Tea Meeting of Dissenters on 13th March 1860 when the room was decorated with suitable mottoes and 130 sat down to tea.

Three years later the pub's meeting room was used for an entirely different purpose. The licensee, Mrs Frances Binstead, turned it into a dormitory for the navvies building the railway which was on its way to Amberley. She charged 6d a night for bed and blanket – and woe betide any chap who tried to avoid paying the sixpence by sharing a bed with a friend. Mrs Binstead had them both out of the house and into the night, whatever the weather.

BRIDGE INN: In 1871 William Smart the licensee pleaded guilty before Arundel magistrates to watering the whisky and was fined £2 and ordered to pay 12s costs. He said he had watered it according to a trade book.

Inquests were often held at the Bridge. At one, in September 1872, it was recorded that Elizabeth Merritt 'whilst in the act of tightening her stays' had dropped dead in the bedroom of her house at Houghton bridge. The verdict at an inquest on George Geering was that he had 'died accidentally run over by a train having fallen asleep across the line while in liquor'. He had, it was said, been wassailing with friends. A platelayer named Leggatt gave evidence of finding first a walking stick by the track and then a boot with a foot in it. ...

ANGMERING

LAMB INN: It was a dark and stormy night in 1835 when Worthing magistrate Sir Richard Jones and his wife were returning from dinner with the Earl of Surrey at Surrey House, Littlehampton. They were travelling by post chaise and the post boy, either drunk or asleep, overturned them into Monmares Pond. With difficulty they were extricated from the sunken chaise and, wrapped in blankets fetched from the nearby Lamb, they were driven home to Worthing in a cart. Sir Richard, who was over 80, died soon afterwards. This sad accident happened 15 years before one of the county's longest serving licensees took charge of the inn. On 25th February 1907, Arundel licensing justices congratulated 81-year-old Thomas Wilkinson on the 57th successive renewal of his licence. He did not, however, live long enough to equal or surpass his mother's record. She was licensee of the Half Moon at Northchapel for 61 years.

Thomas Wilkinson moved to Angmering in 1850 with a wife and four children, and quickly established himself as a village character. In his reign seven local clubs made the inn their headquarters; he captained the village cricket team until he was 61; and he hunted regularly with the Crawley and Horsham foxhounds. On the occasion of Queen Victoria's golden jubilee celebrations he supplied the food for 2,000–3,000 people from Angmering and neighbouring villages.

During part of his tenancy a room by the archway leading to the stables of this former coaching inn was used as the village mortuary – the parish church being only a few yards away. When the roof over this wing of the inn was being repaired a small attic room was discovered which was probably the primitive overnight accommodation for the grooms and post-boys in the days when two or three coaches a day clattered into the inn yard.

SPOTTED COW: There has been a building on this site since 1540. It was formerly a butcher's shop and when it became an inn it was a favoured meeting place of smugglers. There is still a mile long track from the sea, but it is now obscured in parts by buildings and undergrowth.

There is one of the few surviving Twisters or Wheels of Fortune in the ceiling of the saloon bar. It is similar to the rotating arrows mounted above numbered discs that were popular fairground games of chance, and was reputedly used by the smugglers to share out their spoils. Twisters or Spinning Jennies as they are frequently, and quite wrongly called, were ceiling mounted to avoid cheating.

ARDINGLY

THE OAK: The house was built in the 14th century and first recorded as an inn in 1625. It still has some fine examples of medieval masonry deeply worn in places where the farmworkers used to sharpen their knives. Part of the bar support is the mast from one of the barges that used to sail the Ouse when it was made navigable in 1812 from Lewes to Ryelands Bridge, a distance of 22 miles. The coming of the railway put an end to the trade along this waterway – but the end was an unusually busy one. Nearly all the stone and bricks to build the Balcombe viaduct which brought the railway to Brighton in 1841 came up the Ouse by barge from Newhaven.

An early licensee and his wife made the public prints in 1779 because their combined ages totalled 179 years. John Page was 89 and his wife, Frances, 90. 'Both enjoy sight, hearing and memory to a surprising degree' reports the *Sussex Weekly Advertiser* on 25th January of that year.

ARUNDEL

NORFOLK ARMS HOTEL: In 1783 the not inconsiderable sum of £7,223 1s 9d was allocated to finish the building of an inn 'on the site of several ruinous and decayed buildings'. The cash came from leases on the Duke of Norfolk's properties in the London parish of St Clement Dane's which amounted to £35,308, most of which went on repairing and altering Arundel Castle.

Until 1831, when the mayor and corporation decided that they could no longer afford it, an annual buckfeast was held here. The Duke of Norfolk, as Lord of the Manor, presented the buck and it was cooked and served on an evening in August. An undated bill for the buckfeast shows it was a fairly costly occasion:

> Dinner £2 2s.; Madeira £1 3s.; negus (port or sherry with hot water, sweetened and spiced) 13s 4d.; port £2 2s.; punch 13s 2d.; beer at dinner 3s 3d.; teas and coffees 17s 10d.; fruit 3s 6d.; supper 9s.; beer at supper 4s 6d.; cards 7s 6d. Total £9 1s 5d.

Queen Victoria stayed at the Norfolk Arms, so did G K Chesterton and Hilaire Belloc. In July 1793 there was a not so welcome visitor. The *Sussex Weekly Advertiser* of that date reports: 'A well dressed young man with a lady attended by a black servant arrived and soon found means to ingratiate

himself with a gentleman of the town so as to get a loan of £250 with which he decamped. He assumed the title of the Earl of Rutlandshire.'

It was difficult for the owners to make much of a commercial success of the Norfolk in the first 25 years of its existence as troops were constantly being quartered there on their way to Portsmouth for embarkation to fight Napoleon. In one year, 1812, a total of 12,000 soldiers stayed there.

BLACK RABBIT: This riverside mecca for thousands of tourists each summer was originally an alehouse patronised by the crews of the craft using the Wey and Arun canal which, between 1816 and 1871 when it became derelict, linked the Channel port of Littlehampton with the Thames and London. John Olliver, in 1804, is the first recorded licensee and his family were at the inn for the next 70 years. In the 1850s it was patronised by the navvies working on the new cut of the Arun, using chalk from the quarry behind the Black Rabbit, and men working on the new railway. It acquired a reputation for drunkenness, fighting and general bad behaviour. Some 50 years later everything had changed. The inn became a popular pleasure garden with archery, croquet and other pleasant pastimes on its lawns. Boat trips on the river were available and there were stables for the horses of the elegant Edwardians who came in their carriages for al fresco afternoons.

Innkeeper Dan Lee in the 1930s and Sam Knight who succeeded him, continued to hire skiffs for anyone prepared to risk the fast flowing Arun. Today a few motor cruisers are moored nearby but there is no jolly boating.

This inn is, reputedly, the only Black Rabbit in the country. No one knows the reason it bears this name. Black rabbits, which exist in the wild, are beloved of gamekeepers because their presence indicates that there are no poachers around – a black rabbit being a more obvious target than a pale brown one. Was the first licensee a superstitious gamekeeper?

BALLS CROSS

STAG INN: The spit on which a horned sheep is roasted whole each Horn Fair Day on nearby Ebernoe Common is kept in the saloon bar of this inn. And every time there is a general or municipal election the 162 voters on the roll come here to cast their votes.

According to local legend a Horn Fair has been held on St James' Day, 25th July, for the past 500 years, with occasional breaks for wars and rumours of wars. Before the 1914–18 conflict the head and horns of the roasted sheep were presented to the Victor Ludorum of the open air sports held on the common. Latterly they have been given to the top run scorer in a cricket match between Ebernoe and a neighbouring village.

No one knows why this tiny community without even a pub of its own should go to the trouble of roasting a whole sheep and hold a sports day in honour of St James. It has been suggested that the Horn Fair is a survival of a pagan fertility rite or that it is a continuation of communal merrymaking so popular in medieval days. Or did it originate from the time when sheep farmers collected the horns from the animals that they had slaughtered during the year and sold them as souvenirs?

The fair lapsed between 1939 and 1947 as there were no unrationed sheep available for roasting and few men left in the villages to compete for the horns. When it was revived in 1948 the Ministry of Agriculture Fisheries and Food would not give permission for a sheep roast. Lord Leconfield came to the rescue with a set of deer's antlers for the top scorer.

Since local government reorganisation in 1974, the Stag has been used as a polling station. It is not the only pub in the Chichester electoral district to be used for this purpose but its picturesque appearance nearly always attracts the television cameras on polling days.

BARNHAM

MURRELL ARMS: This inn, packed with pieces from the past, collected by licensee and historian Mervyn Cutten, was a farmhouse in the 18th century belonging to William Murrell. He died in 1751 and is buried in the nearby parish church. His tombstone bears the inscription:

> Afflictions sore long time I bore
> Physicians were in vain,
> 'Til Death did seize
> And God did please
> To ease me of my pain.

There is a similar inscription on Martha Myott's gravestone in Stanmer churchyard, near Brighton. She died in 1820 so perhaps whoever ordered the inscription had seen William Murrell's at Barnham – or did they just choose it from the same book of suggested epitaphs supplied by the undertaker?

The railway came to Barnham in 1864 providing a link for Bognor Regis on the Brighton to Portsmouth line. The inn, then a beer only house, found business quickly increased and William Murrell's grandson, the licensee in 1866, applied for and was granted a full on licence. Later innkeepers appeared to have time on their hands for one of them, Robert Marshall, was also the village carpenter and in 1878 landlord Henry Hall added a wheelwright's shop to the pub.

To mark the wedding of Prince Charles and Lady Diana Spencer in 1981 Mervyn Cutten set up a game of hopscotch on the green outside the inn. It is marked out with paving slabs with brass numbers set in them and is well patronised by the local children.

BILLINGSHURST

YE OLDE SIX BELLS: This black and white timbered house with its Horsham stone roof and probably the largest stone flagged floor in the county, was originally a farmhouse. Later it became a lodging house for tramps and travellers and finally an inn.

It has a 16th-century iron gravestone as a fireback in the main bar which bears the inscription:

HERE : LIETH : ANE : ꟻORƧTR
DAUGHTER : AND : HEYR : TO
THOMAƧ : GAYNƧ ORD : EƧQUIER
DECEAƧED : XVIII : Oꟻ : IANVARI: 1591
LEAVING : BEHIND : HER : 11 : ƧONEƧ
AND: V : DAVGHTERƧ

This is one of a number of Anne Forster tombstones all used as firebacks around the county. There is one on Anne

Forster's grave in Crowhurst in Surrey which, like all the others, has the 'S's and 'F's upsidedown and reversed. In 1915 one was found in Ardingly, in a cottage near the old ironworks where possibly they were all cast. It is now in the tower of the parish church. Anne Forster was a relative of the Culpepers and Wakehursts of Wakehurst Place and it has been suggested that the iron slabs were placed in the houses she inherited from her father. Or were they just mistakes – an apprentice misplacing the letters S and F in the moulds so that the whole batch had to be discarded?

Some years ago, when the Six Bells was extended, a tile hung wall was stripped to reveal one of the original 16th-century windows, still with the nails in it used to secure the fabric that covered the aperture before glass was in general use for that purpose. It has been restored and preserved as an interesting historical feature.

In modern times the inn has suffered from flooding. In 1968 the landlord Edward Knapper had to be rescued from an upstairs window by Major Leo Gatfield in his dinghy and again in 1981 the drains gave trouble and there was more flooding.

Bognor Regis

ROYAL OAK: A full abstract of the title deeds of this inn going back to the times of Elizabeth I are held by the brewers Ind Coope but perhaps its greatest claim to fame is that it was once owned by Sir Richard Hotham, the hatter from Southwark, who tried to establish Bognor as a resort town in the 18th century. He spent at least £60,000 on schemes to attract the nobility and gentry to the mansion he built at Hotham Park. All his efforts to get George III to stay there failed but after his death in 1792 it was the summer home of Princess Charlotte, daughter of the Prince Regent. Sir Richard's attempts to get Bognor's name changed to Hothampton also failed.

When its days as a coaching inn were over the Royal Oak was acquired by master brewer Richard William Turner and sold by him to Richard Henty in 1879 for the not inconsiderable sum for those days of £1,000.

SHIP INN: This 200-year-old inn was once the meeting place of smugglers and local legend has it that they used to bring up their contraband through an underground passage connecting the inn to the beach. In rough weather the sea water would flood the cellars, so it was said, and as a result the tunnel was filled in and no trace of it remains.

At the end of the 19th century the Ship offered its guests rooms for 1s a night and their luggage would be brought without cost from the station. It also offered good stabling and ponies and traps for hire.

In the census of 1841 it was referred to as an alehouse and it was modernised in the 1930s while still in the family of Edwin Charles Millar, a survivor of the siege of Sebastapol.

STAMPS: Only the name of this recently rebuilt pub gives any indication of its past history. It was previously called the Rising Sun and for 51 years it was run by Richard Sharpe, a fanatical collector of postage stamps.

He had, in all, 5 million stamps with a face value of £80,000. To mark the golden jubilee of Queen Victoria he papered an entire room at the pub with stamps – 2 million of them. The pattern on the ceiling was of a star and the Bognor coat-of-arms and there were various scenes of Empire in stamps on the wall. Any left over from a particular pattern he would stick round the frames of his pictures. It became a huge tourist attraction. People were drawn in by the sign he had painted on one of the outside walls advertising the 'JUBILEE STAMP HOUSE – R. Sharpe's Great Development'. He produced a catalogue of the display and there were picture postcards of the inn with its sign in the 1900s. Mr Sharpe also counted the number of visitors he had to see his stamps – there were 716,890 of them.

The Rising Sun was demolished in 1957. It was rebuilt in 1987.

VICTORIA INN: These premises were probably rebuilt by local architect and estate agent Arthur Smith around 1870 when they were known as the Victoria Hotel. But it is as the Vicuna Hotel that they are featured by H G Wells in his novel, *The Wheels of Chance*, published in 1896. Wells' mother was for some time housekeeper at Uppark and he stayed with her there when a boy and no doubt was taken to the Victoria Hotel for lunch or afternoon tea on visits to Bognor.

BOSHAM

ANCHOR BLEU: This inn, no distance at all from where Earl Harold set sail in 1064 to visit William, Duke of Normandy, is mentioned in a schedule of local taverns published in 1740. It can still be approached from the sea at high tide and there are mooring rings for dinghies in the wall. A favourite spectator sport for the customers is to watch the tide come in – and swamp the cars that visitors have parked on the strand.

Three yachtsmen set off from the quay near the Anchor in September 1971 with the intention of racing to Bridgetown, Barbados – a distance of 5,000 miles – for a barrel of beer put up by licensee Barry Goodinge, and the brewery. The three were Geoffrey Cath, Alan Gick and Nigel Harman and they set off in boats with different coloured hulls – one red, one white, one blue. But as so often happens they ran into the usual Force 8 off Ushant and had to abandon the race. However, there was an eventual winner – 17 years later. Geoffrey Cath finally made it single-handed to Barbados, having gained valuable experience in several Azores races previously. Barry Goodinge had a bottle of champagne waiting for him on his return to Bosham Sailing Club.

In the last war pilots from RAF Tangmere and Thorney Island were regular visitors and so was artist Rex Whistler and Dylan Thomas, author of *Under Milk Wood*, who was living in Bosham at the time. He was not popular with the regulars. Parties would occasionally get a bit out of hand. On one occasion Barry Goodinge, who joined his father at the Anchor in 1942, found a guest had fallen out of a window and landed head first in the water butt.

BRACKLESHAM BAY

LIVELY LADY: Sir Alec Rose, knighted in 1968 for sailing single-handed round the world, was at the opening ceremony of this pub called after the vessel in which he

undertook the voyage. Also there, on 19th December 1969, was Mr S J P Cambridge, first owner and the man who built the *Lively Lady* on the banks of the Hoogly river in Calcutta between 1947 and 1949.

The inn had other sporting connections for some years. A former licensee was boxing referee Roland Dakin who officiated at many world championship fights. He had on display a collection of boxing gloves that famous fighters had presented to him over the years. Naturally he took them with him when he left some eight years ago.

BROADBRIDGE HEATH

SHELLEY ARMS: When Percy Bysshe Shelley, one of the poetic geniuses of the 19th century, was a small boy this former cottage alehouse bore his family's coat of arms on its inn sign. Young Percy, born at nearby Field Place, in 1792, left the village to go to school at the age of 10 and rarely returned before his tragic death in a boating accident in Italy in 1822. He did not get on with his family and kept away from them as much as possible.

The Shelley Arms was considerably extended in Victorian times and many of its original beams were covered with plaster. It has been fairly recently renovated and the earlier structure again revealed. The reopening in 1984 was marked by a helicopter landing in the back garden and a re-enactment of some of the battles of the Civil War by members of the Sealed Knot Society. It has also staged the world's first Ferret Racing Championships, arranged by a regular customer, Harold Tourle, known locally as 'H'. He is a noted member of the Ferret Fancy.

Bucks Green

FOX INN: A right of way went in one door and out of the other until it was diverted in the 1930s. It existed because in the 16th century there were three cottages on the site and the footpath went between them. As the alehouse which occupied one of the cottages was extended it took in the path and the next cottage. But villagers continued to exercise their right of passage and used to wander through the bar with their horses, barrows, carts and what have you. Occasionally, even today, the odd motorcycle or pony passes through – but that is not by right any longer, but by consent of the licensee.

Burgess Hill

KINGS HEAD: An eccentric landlord called Pagden once ran this inn and he was a guide, comforter and friend to the rogues and vagabonds that haunted it. They must have been too much for him because he hanged himself in the stables at the back of the inn. Another innkeeper, according to the *Story of Burgess Hill* by Albert H Gregory, was Mr Hubbard and he was succeeded by Mr Pronger who wore a Sussex roundfrock or smock when he was behind his bar. Thomas Budd, who held the licence from 1874, stipulated in his will that he wished to be buried in the garden of the Kings Head. He nearly made it – he was laid to rest in the burial ground of St John's chapel, just over the hedge from his garden.

In 1887, when the innkeeper was Charles Tomsett, a dinner was held there for the members of the Burgess Hill Fox

Terrier Rabbit Coursing Club after a successful meeting at which there were 60 dogs entered in the nine events on the card.

CRICKETERS: This inn, called after the summer game, had a brief spell of being called the Fairfield Arms. It was during those days that its regulars were surprised to hear on the wireless Lord Haw Haw making a wartime announcement from Germany that Burgess Hill aerodrome had been bombed by the Luftwaffe. Their surprise was occasioned by the fact that there was no aerodrome at Burgess Hill. 'He must mean Biggin Hill' they decided and left it at that.

The Cricketers had its own cricket team – which used to play regular fixtures with the Brighton Clowns on the Fairfield recreation ground. The Burgess Hill Cricket Week was quite an occasion and among visiting players was C Aubrey Smith, later a British film star in Hollywood but then a class cricketer and, incidentally, the captain of the Burgess Hill Football Club in the 1890s. Another famous player was Vallance Jupp, who was born at Burgess Hill in 1891 and scored 28 and made two brilliant catches in his debut for Sussex against Essex in 1909. His parents, Mr and Mrs George Jupp, ran the Friars Oak at Hassocks in the 1930s.

BURPHAM

GEORGE AND DRAGON: This inn was originally an alehouse run by successive members of the West family – and it remained in the same ownership until the Depression years of the 1930s forced its sale to Arundel brewers Henty and Constable. But the Wests stayed on as tenants and when the last man of the family, George West, died his sisters Ada and Gertie took on the tenancy. Their deaths in 1945 closed a 350-year long phase in the inn's history. But the memory of Big George West lingers on. He was also the village blacksmith and carrier and this mighty man kept order in his pub by the simple expedient of banging his fist on the tap room table when there was trouble and shouting 'remember, that's sudden death'. The chaps preparing for a punch-up would take one look at the vast fist and leave quietly.

Most inns in out of the way places are said to have been the haunt of smugglers. Certainly the George and Dragon is conveniently near the fast flowing Arun along which contraband could be brought up from the coast. Perhaps the Wests themselves found it a profitable sideline for in the mid 18th century, when smuggling was a booming business, they built on a rear extension. It had to be 5 feet lower than the original house because of the steep slope of the hillside. The Twister or spinning jenny in the ceiling of the taproom, now the saloon bar, also indicates that the inn had a smuggling past. This one has Roman numerals and is divided into 10 sections rather than the usual 12.

BURY

BLACK DOG AND DUCK: It was demand for dinners that caused Mr and Mrs Henley to turn their house and its adjoining shop into an inn. The demand came from the navvies working on the railway's Arundel to London line in the 1860s. To begin with Mrs Henley gave them bread and cheese to take to work and cooked them a substantial evening meal. 'Can we have some beer with it, please?' they asked, so the Henleys applied for the house's first licence.

It was originally called the Black Dog and the sign was a portrait of the family's retriever Jim. But Mr Henley was a fine shot and was often out with Jim over the brooks after wild duck so the regulars suggested in jest that such a bird should be added to the sign. It was.

CHARLTON

THE FOX GOES FREE: Between 1670 and 1750 Charlton was the most famous fox hunting village in England and the Charlton Hunt Club numbered among its members and visitors William III, the Grand Duke of Tuscany, the Duke of Monmouth before his defeat at Sedgemoor, the Dukes of Richmond, Devonshire, Bolton, Grafton, Montrose, St Albans Kingston and Montagu and hosts of assorted barons and earls. The members of the hunt slept at Foxhall, a hunting box in the village designed by the Earl of Burlington and no doubt drank at the L-shaped flint pub which was then called the Pig and Whistle. In 1750 the hunt and its kennels moved to Goodwood, where members had the idea of setting up the Goodwood Races, and the Fox as it was then called, lost many of its aristocratic customers. In the 1880s the then landlord tried to get them back. He was a former Colour Sergeant Major in the Royal Engineers and he advertised widely that his house was 'in view of Goodwood Racecourse, about one mile from the grandstand, and one and a half miles from Singleton Station. First class accommodation for visitors. Bean feasts and private parties catered for.'

It was draught horses rather than race horses which brought tragedy to John Kennett, licensee of the Fox from 1890. His son, Walter, was killed at Croydon when the horses on his brewer's dray bolted and he was trampled trying to stop them.

In 1915 the Fox had a woman licensee, Mrs F Laishley, and it was with her encouragement that the first Women's Institute to be formed in England met at the pub on 9th November. The Singleton and East Dean WI continues to flourish and the inn carries a plaque recording its formation. The inn was until recently a tied house. The new name is indicative of its return to free house status.

CHICHESTER

There have been a lot of changes in this cathedral city since the Second World War and many of its old alehouses have gone for good. The ones that are left have also undergone many changes. For instance the Dolphin and Anchor, the three star hotel opposite the cathedral, was two separate establishments until 1910 – the Whig Dolphin and the Tory Anchor.

THE DOLPHIN: Two people connected with this inn died tragically, others lived long lives full of incident. First to go was chaise driver Richard Pulter. In March 1763 he hanged himself in the hayloft above the stables at the back of the inn. In 1813 the new landlord, 27-year-old Charles Triggs dropped dead in his own bar only about 12 hours after a splendid party to welcome him to the Dolphin.

The Dolphin and the Anchor, then separated by a small shop, were in constant competition for coach customers. In 1792 landlord John Parsons advertised in the *London Star* that he 'took the utmost pains to provide the best liquors and a good larder, genteel carriages and able horses. Gentlemen and ladies travelling in post chaises are particularly desired to order their postillions to DRIVE TO THE DOLPHIN for various arts are used to cause them to do otherwise!'

One of these genteel carriages had a nasty accident a few

years later. It was one of those dark and stormy nights and the driver from the Dolphin, Reuben Benham, great grandfather of H G Wells, steered a post chaise into a wharf at Midhurst instead of over the bridge. Wells refers to this incident in his *Experiment with Autobiography* (1912). Another literary connection, also of a physically dramatic nature, was a bare fist fight between poet and novelist George Meredith and Sussex county cricketer H M Hyndman. It was described as a 'rough and tumble' and Meredith was the winner.

The fight, surprisingly, took place at the inn when Mr and Mrs William Ballard were in charge. They took it over in 1838 and ran it as a most orderly house. Mrs Ballard was the sister of Dr Osborn, president of the Wesleyan Conference, and she and her husband helped to establish the Wesleyan chapel in Chichester. She was also the last person to travel around the city in a sedan chair, which she did until her death in 1874.

The Dolphin's allegiance to the Liberal cause began around 1810 when politician and banker John Abel Smith built on an assembly room as a meeting place for his supporters. It became known as the Blue Club and William Stephen Poyntz, the local MP, dined with its members there on 22nd October 1829.

During the Napoleonic wars part of the inn was used as an armoury by the West Sussex Local Militia and its men were billeted there. In 1942 Canadian troops preparing for the raid on Dieppe were there.

THE ANCHOR: Robert Earle held the license of this inn from 1794 until he was succeeded in 1814 by his son-in-law William Coombes, husband of his daughter Maria. His elder daughter, Sarah, had married William Shayer, a landscape painter and their son, born at Chichester in 1811, was to become the famous coaching artist, William Joseph Shayer.

William Coombes has a strange claim to fame – he had a parrot which shared its food and its cage with a cat. Two pewter mugs, inscribed 'W. COOMBES. ANCHOR INN' turned up in a street market in Cairo in 1935. They are now on display in the entrance hall of the hotel.

Anchor landlords were only too keen to poach the Dolphin's carriage trade. In 1826 the *Hampshire Telegraph* carried this advertisement: 'The public are respectfully informed that the Independence Post Coach is removed from the Dolphin Inn to the original offices at the Anchor, Chichester, where the proprietors trust the same patronage will be stowed on them as heretofore.'

It was from the steps of this inn that a Light Horseman fired his carbine at the weathercock on the 277-feet high spire of the cathedral. He scored a direct hit on this gilded cockerel made by Daniel Seymour in 1638 and it bears the scars to this day.

ROYAL ARMS: Queen Elizabeth I held audiences in an upper room when this inn was Scarborough House, the country home of her friend and adviser Lord Lumley. The 'royal room', ornamented with mouldings done by 16th-century Italian craftsmen, has been carefully preserved as part of the private apartments of the premises. Until the 18th century, when it was converted to a shop, the east wing was the parsonage of St Mary's School. One of its beams is inscribed with the name WILLIAM HOLLAND, the founder of Steyning School and a 16th-century mayor of Chichester.

At the beginning of the 19th century a Mr Parker bought the pub and started to make the milk punch for which it is still renowned. The massive cask Mr Parker used to advertise his product is still on display and his successor John Hudson was appointed Manufacturer of Punch in Ordinary to Queen Victoria.

The milk punch tradition has been continued by the present licensee, Mr Dennis Pordage. When the Queen came to the cathedral in 1987 to distribute the Maundy money he was there to present her with a bottle of milk punch which he had made in one week from the original recipe. He later received a letter from Windsor saying that Her Majesty had thoroughly enjoyed it. 'I hope she had it heated up' said Mr Pordage. 'The heat brings out the flavour of the brandy and other ingredients that go into the milk'.

SHIP HOTEL: This Georgian house was formerly the home of Admiral Sir George Murray (1759–1819) which presumably is the reason it is so named. It was a private house and then an antique shop and was granted a licence just before the Second World War. Some very top brass moved in before D Day and it is likely that Allied Commander in Chief, General Dwight D Eisenhower, and Allied Chiefs of Staff, including Field Marshal Montgomery and Air Chief Marshal Sir Arthur Tedder discussed plans for the Allied invasion of Europe on the premises.

CHILGROVE

ROYAL OAK: Around the turn of the century, when Alfie and Carrie Ainger ran this isolated country pub near what is now the South Downs Way, they had a royal visitor. King Edward VII dropped in for a drink while out shooting over the 11,000 acres of the West Dean estate belonging to rich American Willie James and his wife, Evelyn. The King's signature is in the game book of a three day shoot in November 1896 when the total bag was 3,241 made up of 3,010 pheasants, seven partridges, 92 hares, 129 rabbits and three woodcock.

Alfie Ainger was a true countryman. When asked by the licensing justices about the sanitary arrangements at the Royal Oak he replied: 'But, sir, I have nine acres.'

CHRIST'S HOSPITAL

BAX CASTLE: Why this former village beerhouse bears the name and carries on its sign the coat of arms of a Master of the King's Musick concerned readers of the *West Sussex County Times* for several weeks in the winter of 1983. It all started on the centenary of the birth of composer Sir Arnold Bax when the paper observed that he had given his name to a Sussex pub.

'Not so' said Mr David Francis of Barns Green Farm, in the next edition. He said he was born at the pub and so had been his mother and grandmother before him. It had been called the Bax Castle for at least 100 years – after a local weaver called John Bax. His mother's maiden name was Beatrice Annie Gratwick. Another point he made was that locally the pub was known as the Donkey because there was always one in the paddock nearby.

A fortnight later Miss Mary Greaves of Horsham entered the debate. She had been instrumental in getting a plaque put up on the White Horse at Storrington commemorating the fact that Sir Arnold lived there for 11 years until his death in 1953. She claimed that the composer did not know of the existence of the Bax Castle until he was taken there by a friend from Christ's Hospital in the late 1940s or early 50s.

A search through the parish records of Itchingfield produced a yeoman called William Bax who had a copse named after him and a weaver called John Bax who in 1799 received 11s 3d for 30 ells of cloth. In A J Smith's *Seventy Years in Southwater* the inn is said to be tenanted by a member of the Bax family, also a weaver 'but is still referred to as the Donkey'.

Street directories make no mention of the name Bax Castle until 1938 when the landlord was Frank Lionel Sleight. Edward Gratwick, beer retailer, Two Mile Ash appears from 1899–1922. He was succeeded by William James Francis, beer retailer and in 1934 Leonard J Stater is listed.

The reason for the name becomes clearer when Sir Arnold's ancestry is investigated. Writing in the *Sussex County Magazine* in 1953 Mr John Wright traces the family back to yeomen farmers in the Capel and Ockley area in 1655. That is no distance from Itchingfield where Yeoman William Bax was living in 1724, so a close family connection can be presumed. And in 1937 Arnold Bax was knighted and acquired his own coat of arms. In 1938 his arms and the name were on the pub.

COCKING

RICHARD COBDEN: This 18th century inn acquired its present name in the late 19th century in honour of the apostle of free trade and founder of the Anti-Corn Law League who was born in a farmhouse in the village in 1804. Everywhere around Cocking Richard Cobden is remembered. Dunford House, which he built on the site of his birthplace, is now a conference centre and near it is an obelisk to his memory. In the pub is framed the story of his life and work.

Richard Cobden was the fourth of 11 children and he spent five years at Dotheboys Hall. Not surprisingly, after that experience, he did all he could to save the starving. He worked so hard for free trade that he came near to bankruptcy from which he was only saved by public subscription. He and other workers for the league travelled the country urging repeal of the protectionist measures on corn and their victory came after the 1845 failure of the Irish potato crop. Cobden was an able statesman and it was he who negotiated a Treaty of Commerce with France which had the effect of removing heavy duties on French silks and wine. From 1860, when the treaty was signed, cheap French wines began to come into this country.

COWFOLD

HARE AND HOUNDS: The local charcoal burner once lived in this 200-year-old house which in the late 19th century was the canteen and temporary hostel for the English, French, German and Belgian stonemasons and other craftsmen building the nearby monastery of St Hugh Charterhouse.

The foundation stone of the monastery was laid on 17th October 1877 and the architects were Cloves, Norman and Sons from Calais. Local quarries supplied most of the stone but some came from Bath. Every fortnight 60,000 bricks were made at four kilns on the site and some 700 workmen were kept busy on the project for several years. As the pub was in no way big enough to accommodate even half this number a single storey extension was built onto it to provide a form of mess hall. It was demolished after the First World War. The monastery has 34 cells in the cloisters for the fathers and 32 rooms for the lay brothers. It is of the Carthusian order established by St Bruno of Cologne in 1084.

After this 19th-century burst of business the Hare and Hounds returned to being a quiet village inn. It became, and still is, the headquarters of the Cowfold Football Club and it was not until the mid 1960s, when Doug Winters was the licensee, that its beer licence was changed to a full on licence.

CRAWLEY

GEORGE HOTEL: When Henry Waller was the licensee of this inn, which dates from 1615 according to the inscription on the fireplace, it was sold to a judge. It was part of the manor of Crawley which was bought in 1671 by Sir William Morton from Sir John Covert of Slaugham.

It became a recognised halfway house for coaches from London to Brighton and often the famous yellow barouche belonging to the Prince of Wales was in its courtyard. Charles James Fox, Whig statesman and pal of the Prince was a frequent visitor as was playwright Richard Brinsley Sheridan. Almost every bare-fisted fighter of note stayed at the George before their bouts at Crawley Down and Colonel Mellish, the great Regency gambler, stopped his coach here and drank his bottle.

Another regular was gentleman coachman Sir John Lade who often gave lunch to his wife, a fine looking woman who was a cook before becoming one of the belles of London society. And the coaches kept on coming, as many as 50 a day would change horses here and it was not until 1887 that the last postboy was paid off.

Some slur must have been cast upon the equestrian facilities the George had to offer in 1797 for on 3rd July of that year the landlord Edward Anscombe announced in the *Sussex Weekly Advertiser* that he was 'much injured by false reports being circulated that he had not got any post horses.' He begged to contradict this by saying he 'had never been without post horses for these 18 years and at this time has as clean chaises and as good horses as any between London and Brighton.'

A Rowlandson print dated 1789 shows the George with its gallows type sign stretching across the road and an auctioneer selling a horse beneath it. The sign, somewhat altered, still stretches right across the road but there is no auctioneer and no horse.

THE ROCKET: This was formerly the Railway Hotel and it was here, on 30th July 1866, that Mark Lemon, the first editor of *Punch*, called a meeting to found the Crawley Volunteer Fire Brigade. There was another meeting a fortnight later at which he announced that his friend Thomas Bronsfield, had sent a fire engine from London with which to fight the fires in the neighbourhood.

A little while later the brigade with its new engine was rushing to a fire when a farm waggon loaded with manure crossed the road. There was a collision and some of the firemen were flung into the dung. For many years Mark Lemon's son-in-law Mr T H Martin was surgeon to the fire brigade.

CRAWLEY DOWN

THE PRIZEFIGHTERS: This village pub was called the Brickmakers Arms until the 1960s when it was refurbished and decorated with boxing memorabilia associated with the career of Freddie Mills, the British and Empire Light Heavyweight Champion who was also World Champion at this weight from 1948 until beaten by Joey Maxim in 1950. Shortly before his suspicious death in 1965 (he was found shot dead in his car in a London street) Freddie Mills was guest of honour at the re-opening.

There were no houses on Crawley Down 150 years ago when the natural amphitheatre formed by the terrain was the scene of many a bloody bare-fisted bout. One of the most celebrated lasted for only one round – but what a round. Jack Randall, the nonpareil, got hold of the head of Master of the Rolls, baker Jack Martin, clamped it under his arm and punched away at it until Martin fell to the ground. That scrap took place in 1821. Three years earlier the poet John Keats was among the spectators when a 34 round contest took place. He had been brought by friends who were hoping to distract him from his grief over the death of his 19-year-old brother, Tom.

CUCKFIELD

KING'S HEAD: In the 18th century this was a busy coaching inn and was on occasions used as a kind of casualty clearing station for travellers injured in accidents on the London to Brighton coach road. In 1819 the Coburg coach, on its way to London, overturned at Cuckfield killing one passenger and injuring a number of others. The horses had been changed at the King's Head but the leaders started off in an unruly fashion, according to a contemporary account, and the coach collided with a waggon. A Mr Blake, described as 'a well known London gentleman' died next day, another had his arm broken, and five had to remain at the inn 'which was turned into a hospital, not for the first time.'

The main London to Brighton road no longer passes the front door of the inn but the fine Act of Parliament Clock is still in the saloon bar, ready to be consulted by travellers. It was made by Smiths of Cuckfield in 1797 when Parliament imposed a levy of five shillings on every clock and watch. To avoid paying this tax people sold their personal timepieces and relied on communal clocks to tell the time. The clocks always had large unglazed faces so they could be seen from a distance without the distortion of reflections on the glass. Customers of the nearby Talbot Inn were charged a penny a time by successive landlords of the Kings Head to consult the clock in the bar.

Around this time there was some local unease about the radical views expressed by Tom Paine and the French Revolutionaries. The Cuckfield establishment took it all very seriously. On 13th February 1792 Francis Sergison of Cuckfield Park took the chair at a meeting of the local landed gentry at the inn. They set up a Society of Friends of King and Constitution with the avowed aim of 'discussing and suppressing the publication of all unconstitutional or republican doctrines tending to overturn the present happy establishment.'

TALBOT: The upper rooms of this former coaching inn were used as a courthouse until January 1888 when the new court house was built at Haywards Heath. And it was here, in 1759, the second Volunteer movement in Sussex was started. These Volunteers were troops of local militia first raised when Britain was drawn into the Seven Years War. Many more such troops were set up during the Napoleonic Wars.

DELL QUAY

CROWN AND ANCHOR: In the 16th century this was the third major grain port in the south-east and the premises that now form the inn were the sleeping quarters of the seamen and labourers who used to work here. At the time of the Roman occupation it was probably a tavern for the Roman legions for in those days it was also an important port. Now it has silted up and the shallows have been turned into a wildfowl reserve.

It was across these shallows, which were then a little deeper, that the smugglers came bringing contraband from France. Local legend says that on one occasion five Revenue men were murdered by the smugglers in the cellars of the inn and that years later some bodies were found buried in the garden. The local vicar was reputedly the leader of the smuggling gang. No names or dates have been found in the records to corroborate these tales.

The inn was at one time a Customs House – a change from being a smugglers' safe house – and ring-the-bull is still played here, on a real bull's head.

DONNINGTON

SELSEY TRAM: A bit of romantic railway history survives in the name of this modern pub. It was near here that Selsey Light Tramway, opened in August 1897, crossed the Chichester to Witterings road on its 7 mile run to Selsey.

The plan behind the project was to open up the Hundred of Manhood. Once this was a heavily timbered area (i.e. Main Wood – Manhood) which previously had to rely on horse transport only.

The Tramway was built as cheaply as possible and in 1910 suffered from serious flooding as the result of a storm which had raged for days. It had one fatal accident. Fireman Arthur Baines was crushed against the boiler of the *Chichester* locomotive by the buffer of the first coach and killed instantly when the train jumped the tracks near the golf club halt.

After the First World War traffic on the tramway declined. Even the introduction of two Shefflex rail cars powered by four cylinder petrol engines and built on Model T Ford bus chassis did not help. Competition from road transport was just too much – the trains travelled so slowly that cyclists used to race against them and win. In January 1935 the railway closed for good. Now only the name remains.

DRAGON'S GREEN

GEORGE AND DRAGON: In front of this village inn is a gravestone in the shape of a cross with this sad inscription: 'In loving memory of Walter, the Albino son of Alfred and Charlotte Budd. Born February 12, 1869, died February 18, 1893. May God forgive those who forgot their duty to him who was just and afflicted.'

Parishioners and parents have different versions of the reason for Walter's suicide. The parishioners claimed that his mother treated him so badly that he killed himself. The parents said that the young man was unjustly accused of a petty crime and this so preyed on his mind that he drowned himself. Subsequent events support the parents' claim.

Walter was buried in Shipley churchyard and no sooner had

the stone mason finished the inscription on the tombstone than Mrs Budd was asked by the vicar, the Reverend Henry Gorham, to have the last part deleted. She refused but the parishioners put such pressure on her that in the end she moved the whole tombstone, with its inscription intact, to the front of the inn kept by her husband. This was not the end of the matter. Friends of the family, who had placed wreaths on Walter's grave in the churchyard, found they had been removed by the new vicar, the Reverend Edward Arkle. Mrs Budd put up a notice recording this fact on the tombstone outside the inn.

The tombstone is still there and has been listed as a monument of historic interest.

DUNCTON

CRICKETERS' ARMS: This 16th-century inn, formerly a brewery, was known as the Swan until 1867 when it was bought by John Wisden, publisher of that famous yellow-covered *Cricketers' Almanac.* He installed as his tenant the father of James Dean, the Sussex and England cricketer, who was instrumental in getting round arm bowling recognised. This style of delivery, in which the ball is brought up to shoulder height, is transitional between original under-arm bowling and the present day over-arm style. Dean's deliveries were effective. On two occasions he took eight wickets in an innings, once against Kent in 1851 and against the MCC in 1855.

His portrait is on one side of the inn's sign. On the other is the Master himself – Dr W G Grace.

EASTERGATE

WILKES HEAD: The people of Sussex took a great fancy to revolutionary John Wilkes in the last years of the 18th century. This Whig politician championed the cause of the people and for a ferocious attack on the Government in his paper, the *North Briton,* he was sent to the Tower. He talked his way out and bounced back after several expulsions from the House of Commons. In the end the establishment gave up on him and he was made Lord Mayor of London and, in 1779, Chamberlain of the City of London. His morals were not exactly immaculate. The Duke of Marlborough said to him: 'You'll either die on the gallows or die of the pox' to which Wilkes, the wit, replied: 'It depends, my lord, on whether I embrace your principles – or your mistress.'

This lovable lad made a kind of royal progress through Sussex in 1770. At Chichester there was a splendid reception for him on his release from the Tower and the Market Cross was illuminated by 45 lbs of candles and those who did not join in the general rejoicing had their windows broken.

The pub that bears Wilkes name was built in 1746 and became an inn in 1803 – six years after our hero died.

EAST GRINSTEAD

DORSET ARMS: A collection of painted panels from the coaches that used to call are retained at this Berni steakhouse. It was a recognised halt between London and Brighton and the pioneer of Brighton coaching, James Batchelor, who died in 1763, was its landlord. His widow carried on both the coaching business and the inn until she died in 1817. James Batchelor was the owner of the New Machine which, he told the world in a poster, would run three times a week from the George Inn, Haymarket to East Grinstead. Lewes and Brighton 'if God Permit'. The fare was 16 shillings inside, 8 shillings outside, including 14lbs of luggage per passenger.

In the coaching days and afterwards it had some famous guests. Spencer Perceval, the Prime Minister who was assassinated in the lobby of the House of Commons, was a frequent visitor and so too was Perdita Robinson, a society beauty who would call for lunch on her way to Brighton and the arms – and the bed – of the Prince of Wales. She never paid her bills and they were eventually settled by the State. Royal guests included the Princess Victoria and her mother, the Duchess of Kent. In 1918 the Grand Duke Michael of Russia, fleeing from the revolution, stayed there for eight months.

The inn was originally called the New Inn and later the

Ounce – an Asiatic animal of the cat family and allied to the leopard. A leopard figures in the Sackville coat of arms, hence the name, but colloquially it was called the Cat – heraldic leopards looking very like cats with spots on to the zoologically naive. A token issued by the inn's proprietor during the Commonwealth bears the inscription: 'At the Catt in East Grinstead. 1650. T.E.P.'

The first East Grinstead County Court was held at the Kings Arms in 1847 and ten years later 'Court Hand in Hand' of the Ancient Order of Foresters was inaugurated on the premises.

CROWN HOTEL: William Payne, innkeeper here in 1793, was also the town's Excise Officer and set up an Excise Office at the inn. Another licensee prepared to do his civic duty was William Head who was on the Fire Brigade Committee from 1863. The formation of the brigade was celebrated with a dinner at the Crown and for years the engine was kept in the yard at the back of the inn.

The last court leet of the Manor of Imberhorne was held here in 1886 when the only tenant who appeared to do homage and be sworn in on a silver rod was Mr Head of Kingscote Nursery.

Today the Crown is a plush two star hotel. In 1811 it was let at £30 a year – and a farm went with it.

East Wittering

ROYAL OAK: It was in the barn and stables attached to this inn that the bodies of seamen and the passengers washed ashore from the ships wrecked on the Hounds, a group of rocks off Selsey Bill, were laid out for inspection by the coroner in the 18th and 19th centuries.

In those days there were farmers and fishermen in the area. Now it is a holiday home for many people, attracted by the excellent bathing from the sandy beach.

For 42 years the Steel family ran the pub and from the 1920s, when the holidaymakers began to turn up in quantity, they advertised lunches, teas, bathing huts to let – and new laid eggs.

ELSTED

BALLARDS: A short time after 1864, when the Midhurst to Petersfield branch line was constructed, the Railway Inn was built almost next door to the station at Elsted. Train passengers, villagers and other visitors called in for rest and refreshment until 1955 when the line was closed. Then they had to come by car, coach, cycle – or on foot.

There have been some changes in the last decade. The beer has been brewed on the premises for the past eight years – and the name has been changed.

When solicitor Mike Brown and his wife, Carola, went to the British Beer Exhibition in London what they saw there convinced them that one man breweries were viable. So they set one up in the stables of the Railway Inn. They had a bit of a problem about the name. Brown Ales did not sound quite right so they settled for Carola's maiden name, Ballard, and Ballards Brewery was born. And the Railway Inn's name was changed to Ballards. This was not the first time that name has been over a brewery in Sussex. Until 1924, when it was bought out by a Croydon firm, there was a Ballards Brewery at Southover in Lewes, East Sussex. 'Perhaps a distant relative' said Carola, who is soon to put the historical clock back and become an alewife as so many women did in the 15th, 16th and 17th centuries. Ballards Brewery is soon to move to a nearby industrial estate and head brewer Mike is going back to being a solicitor and Carola is taking over his job. At present they brew beer for some 45–50 pubs in Sussex, Surrey and Hampshire.

FAYGATE

FROG AND NIGHTGOWN: Not a lot has happened to change this old farm workers alehouse over the years except that its name has been changed and it now has a full on licence instead of beer sales only. The front room and hall of a semi-detached cottage still form the bar – but no longer of the Royal Oak. When a new licensee took over in 1980 he changed the name because he thought there were too many Royal Oaks around the county. He decided to be the one and only Frog and Nightgown – in Sussex anyway. There is one in London's Old Kent Road.

FELPHAM

THE FOX: Most of this 18th-century inn and all its thatched roof was destroyed in a disastrous fire in the 1940s but it has been sympathetically restored. A work of art went up in those flames. George Morland, who died in 1804 from alcoholic poisoning, was staying at Felpham with his friend, poet and biographer William Hayley and popped into the Fox for a few drinks. As he could not pay for them he painted a mural on the wall of the bar to settle his account. That wall, and others, are now covered with oak panelling from Colonel Arthur Henty's home, Oaklands Park, in Chichester. For the Fox used to belong to Henty and Constable's brewery, which was responsible for the restoration work after the fire.

Visionary poet and artist William Blake lived in a cottage opposite the inn between 1800 and 1803. Here he wrote Jerusalem and also ejected a couple of drunken soldiers from his garden with the words: 'Damn the King, damn all his subjects, damn his soldiers for they are all slaves.' For this outburst Blake was charged with treason and tried at the Assizes in Chichester. He was acquitted and soon afterwards left Felpham for good.

The Fox has a double inn sign. Above a painting of a prowling fox is a wrought iron sign of the Revenue cutter, the *Fox*, which plied the Channel in pursuit of smugglers in the 18th century.

FERNHURST

RED LION: Parish registers record an innkeeper in the village in 1592. Perhaps he owned the Red Lion. By 1621 it was in the hands of William Fynche and his wife and they were brought before the bishop on one of his visitations for 'selling of drink in praying time.'

Title deeds of the Red Lion show that it was owned in 1699 by George Osbourne of Surrey, Gent., who granted it to Robert Purse to be held of the Lord of the Manor of Diddlesford for 1,000 years at a peppercorn rent.

It became known as Purse's House for it was obviously in the same family for many years. A 19th-century deed describes it as 'heretofore called or known as Purse's house but then commonly called the Red Lion'.

Ferring

TUDOR CLOSE: Some local guide books say this thatched converted tithe barn is mentioned in the Domesday Book. It is not. The entry for Ferring mentions 15 villagers, 14 smallholders, one slave, four pigs, meadows and woodland. There is no mention of a barn or house of any sort.

Tudor Close was for a time the home of composer Paul Rubens who wrote some of the numbers for *Floradora* in 1899 and then topped the charts with the music for *Miss Hook of Holland* which ran for 462 performances at the Prince of Wales Theatre from 1907. In 1910 he had another successful musical, *The Balkan Princess*, written by Frederick Lonsdale and Frank Curzon and in 1915 he wrote the music for *Tonight's the Night*. Paul Rubens moved from Ferring to Worthing and then to Falmouth where he died in 1917.

Tudor Close was turned into a boys preparatory school between the wars and the headmaster was Herbert Noel Cook. During the Second World War, when the school was evacuated, it became the brigade headquarters officers' mess for the Canadians stationed in the area. The school came back after VE Day but did not prosper and the premises were bought by brewers, Ind Coope, in 1947.

Successive owners have added various features to the interior of the old building. There is a lamp standard which was once part of a Tudor four-poster bed and the elaborately carved fireplace in the main bar is of Eastern origin – an import of the brewers. A faded and extremely frail old Flemish tapestry of a French hunting scene hangs on a wall. There is another exactly like it at Hampton Court, 'That is the copy, ours is the original' insists licensee Clive Brown.

FINDON

GUN INN: Part of this inn was a gunsmith's shop in 1722, hence its name. An inventory taken in that year for William Lasseter has survived and describes the premises as consisting of a hall, two parlours, two kitchens, seven bedchambers, a brewhouse, a buttery, milkhouse, scullery, workroom, gunsmith's shop and cellars. Another inventory, made 22 years later for a new tenant, William Parsons, lists the same accomodation but with one difference – instead of a gunsmith's shop there is a dining room.

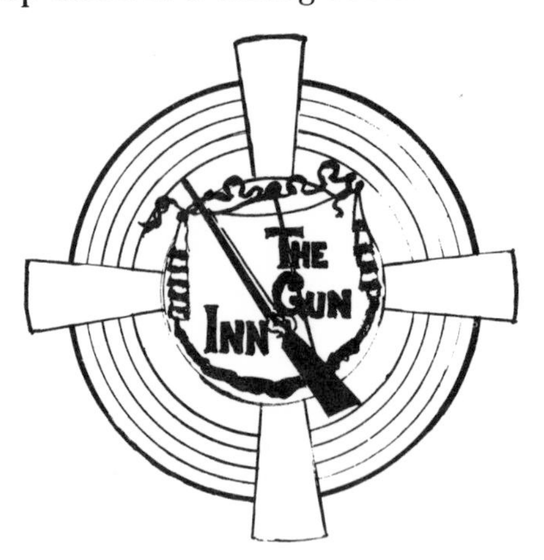

On a summer Sunday afternoon in 1792 a traveller from London arrived in Findon and made straight for the Gun. What he found there is recorded in *Fragments of Findon* by H R P Wyatt (1926) which quotes the anonymous traveller's diary. 'A cold pigeon pye and the mangled remains of a piece of beef was all the inn afforded. Our landlord was civil and inclined to accommodate and a butcher's shop was near but that resource availed us not. Therefore with hunger the very best sauce we sat down and agreed that even the beef was good in its then worst of all states, neither hot or cold. Our host's daughter was drawn out vastly fine, all in white, which we presently discovered was on the occasion of a funeral of a neighbour's child which its mother, poor woman, had unfortunately overlaid.'

Five years later the inn was owned by the local vicar, the Reverend William French. As licensee he took out a £450 insurance policy against fire with the Sun Insurance Company and this firm's plaque is still on the premises. It needed to be on show so the firemen of the day would put the fire out – knowing they would get paid for doing so.

In the 19th century visitors to the Gun were usually members of the sporting fraternity. The village had become, and still is, a centre for the training of racehorses and a Derby winner was once stabled at the inn. It was *Kermit*, ridden to victory at Epsom in 1867 by Ian Goater, cousin of the innkeeper and trainer, William Goater.

FITTLEWORTH

SWAN INN: There were two alehouses in the village in 1536, one of them no doubt being the Swan. The first mention of its name is in a 1640 inquisition taken on the death of Thomas Stanley. Mail coaches stopped here on their way between London and the coast to change horses until the early years of the 19th century when they were followed by the artists.

It was Vicat Coles, who rented a large house called Brinkwells in the village, who brought the painters to the place – and the pub. He gave sketching classes there and, as he had a wide circle of friends in the art world, they would come down to stay with him in the country. At the Swan was Miss Jane Hawkins, whose father, George, had the inn before her. She

liked art and artists and encouraged them to come to the house – and to paint pictures in it. The result is the present Picture Room which, on its oak panels, has works by John Varley, S G Burgess, R H Shapman, Harold Cheesman, Henry Clark, Henry Charles Clifford, George Constable, Edward Knight, W Stuart Lloyd, Edward Handley Read, Alexander Trotter and Augustus Weedon – to name but a lot.

Also on display is the old gallows type inn sign which used to stretch across the road, in defiance of the Act of Parliament of 1797, which forbade such ostentatious display and hazard to traffic. It was painted by Robert Caton Woodville and his son. Father was an artist who painted scenes of conflict in the Boer War and between them they constructed a sign showing a naked Leda, who looked remarkably like Queen Victoria, sitting on a swan. But word got round that Her Majesty was not amused and the naked Leda was quickly clothed in draperies and turned into a faerie queen. On the reverse of the sign is painted a frog smoking a pipe, a swan with a ring round its neck and a floating tankard.

Another tenant of Brinkwells was composer Edward Elgar

but there is no record of him visiting the Swan. He wrote some string quartets at Fittleworth which later formed the theme of his cello concerto and a group of chamber music bears the inscription 'Brinkwells in 1918'.

FULKING

SHEPHERD AND DOG: After a day up to their waists in water washing their sheep before shearing, shepherds would stagger stiffly into the bar parlour for warmth and for ale, no doubt in that order. From the 14th century until modern times Southdown sheep have been reared on the surrounding Downs. In late May or early June each year the Fulking stream, fed by the spring close to the inn, would be dammed where the road dips to form a sheep wash. The water was icy as it had drained through the downland chalk but two or three men at a time would have to stand in it, one throwing in the sheep, the others washing them and putting them out onto the grass on the other side of the dam. Just a few years before the sheepwash was closed casks were set into the ground so the men could stand in them and get some protection from the cold.

John Ruskin, a writer who took a great interest in promoting the well-being of the people of his times (1819–1900) had the idea of harnessing the waters of the Fulking stream to power a hydraulic ram which would pump the supply around the parish. The little Gothic pump house is still there and on it is a plaque bearing an inscription from Psalms 104, 10 and 107, 8.

> 'He sendeth springs into the valleys which run among the hills.
> Oh that men would praise the Lord for his goodness.'

Above the spring itself the Southern Water Authority has put up another plaque. It warns people of the dangers of drinking the water. . . .

The Shepherd and Dog was not always full of wet shepherds. In 1844 the waywarden, the man responsible for the roads in the parish, was Nathaniel Blaker and he had been summonsed to appear before the justices at Steyning over the matter of repairs to Holmbush Lane. He called a protest meeting at the pub and the villagers turned out in force and insisted that the parish was not responsible for the repairs. The matter went to arbitration and Mr Blaker and his supporters won. The justices ruled that Holmbush Lane was on the boundary line and Fulking was not responsible for it.

GOODWOOD

GOODWOOD PARK: The 18th-century Richmond Arms inn is now a luxury hotel but the cockpits around which the sporting gentlemen of an earlier day used to wager vast sums on the fighting qualities of their favourite birds have been preserved. There are three pits – a training ring, smaller practice pit and a large pit. They are lined, as most cockpits were, with the knuckle bones of sheep which provided a good clawhold for the contestants.

It was at the Richmond Arms in 1803 that the stewards of the Goodwood Races, started in the previous year, met to settle their accounts and answer any demand on the General Fund. As a result of the war with France and the 'great failure of subscriptions' they announced that they were not able to give £50 for a handicap sweepstake and that owners would be required to subscribe ten guineas each unless they had won a race at the meeting. If they had they could enter the handicap sweepstake free.

The marble surround to one large fireplace at the Richmond Arms bore the signatures of the jockeys, some famous, others not so famous, who had ridden over the course in the past 100 years. It is still there.

What has gone is the lion figurehead from the Centurion, the ship in which Commodore George Anson circumnavigated the globe between 1740 and 1746. He and his squadron found plunder in Peru and captured a Manila galleon valued at £400,000. The figurehead was presented to the Duke of Richmond but later it was moved to Greenwich at the command of William IV who took a great fancy to it. It stood in the Anson ward of the Royal Naval Hospital from 1834 and was then transferred to the Royal Naval Asylum where it gradually decayed away. On its pedestal in the stable yard of the inn was this inscription:

'Stay Traveller awhile and view
One who has travelled more than you
Quite round the Globe thru ' each degree
Anson and I have ploughed the sea.
Torrid and frigid zones have past
And safe ashore arrived at last;
In ease with dignity appear
He in the House of Lords, I here.'

It was from *The King's Ships* by H S Lecky and it accompanied the lion to Greenwich. Another poet inspired to not particularly good verse by the figurehead was Locker-Lampson. He wrote:

How many dismal years have rolled away
Since I was doomed to premature decay
In utmost need, without a friend on earth
Forced in the King's highway to gain a berth.
I took my stand beside a village inn
For no kind shelter could I find within,
And uncomplaining bore my landlord's prate
The ostler's daily jest, the boor's debate,
To me no voice in soothing accents spoke,
On me the traveller cast his passing joke.'

HANDCROSS

RED LION: On a sunny June day in 1906 the motor omnibus Vanguard was bowling down to Brighton carrying a party of firemen from Orpington and St Mary's Cray on their annual outing. As the bus began the descent of the steep hill into Handcross at a steady 12mph the brakes failed. It quickly gathered speed and hurtled down the hill and crashed into a large oak tree. A number of passengers were flung into the branches of the tree.

In this, the county's first major road accident, eight of the 34 people in the bus were killed instantly, one died a few hours later and a tenth survived for a further two days. It was in the Red Lion, where all the dead and injured had been taken, that the inquest was opened. The coroner, Mr G Vere Benson, asked witnesses to give their evidence quietly as there was a man dying in the next room. Then word was passed to him that the man – William Bailey, headmaster of Chelsfield School, Orpington – had died of his injuries.

On 27th July, three weeks after the tragedy, the full inquest was opened in the garden of the Red Lion – in a marquee supplied by the London Omnibus Company, owners of the Vanguard, the wreck of which was housed in the inn's stables. It ended finally in mid August and the jury's verdict was that no one could be held criminally responsible for the accident. A disaster fund was set up for the families of the victims and among the organisations that subscribed to it was the newly formed Automobile Association. A total of £3,000 was raised.

In the days of the stage coaches the road past the Red Lion was the main route to London from the coast. Often passengers would call there for gin and gingerbread, having walked from Cuckfield, where the London bound coaches stopped for a long time.

'A number of stools and benches were always placed in front of the inn to receive the wearied muscles of the promenaders' writes Shergold in his *Recollections of Brighton in Olden Times*. 'Bannister, the publican, would walk forth from his inn carrying a gallon bottle of gin in one hand and a basket of gingerbread in the other. "You must be tired, gentlemen," he would say. "Come! Take a glass and a slice!"'

In 1908, in spite of the Vanguard tragedy, the Red Lion was still looking to the road for its trade. It carried a sign advertising 'Automobilists and cyclists especially catered for. Tea gardens and bowling green.'

The inn has been modernised fairly recently and now has a carvery and a large dining room offering much more than gin and a slice.

FOUNTAIN: Before he became landlord of this inn a higgler called White narrowly escaped being caught by Police Sergeant Akehurst at the illicit still for making brandy from mangolds that he had set up at nearby Gillhams. Later White took over the Hen and Chickens at Southwater, an appropriate pub for a man of his trade. Higglers were chicken rearers and fatteners and in 1893 7 million chickens were sent to London from the Handcross area.

Another licensee was an old huntsman called Hopkins who used to turn out 'in the pink' whenever hounds met at Handcross.

HASSOCKS

FRIARS OAK: For an inn reputedly 400–500 years old this brick-built tile-hung building looks remarkably Edwardian. And it is. The old Friars Oak inn was on the opposite side of the road and the oak tree after which it was called was near to the site of the present inn which was built in 1905.

Tales are told, but cannot be corroborated, about its origin. There was, it is said, a monastery near where the present inn now stands, and at the entrance to the footpath to Hurstpierpoint was an ancient oak beneath which the monks would sit distributing food to the poor of the parish. This oak reached a circumference of 15ft 6ins before it was struck down.

An oil painting of a monk dancing beneath the oak used to hang in the old inn but it disappeared. It was found by a man from Hurstpierpoint in a London picture gallery and he bought it for a modest sum in 1899 and returned it to the innkeeper, Mr Parker Marchant. It has since disappeared again.

The old inn had the date 1657 carved on the fireplace in one of the bedrooms. The Prince of Wales, later George IV, frequently changed horses here when coaching to Brighton and on one occasion he was snowed up and had to stay the night. Another keen coaching man, James Selby, wagered £1,000 that he would drive the Old Times coach the 108 miles from Brighton to London and back in eight hours. He won his bet with ten minutes to spare, changing horses at the Oak in 60 seconds.

An earlier visitor was John Burgess, a tradesman from Ditchling. He was a Strict Baptist but his diary reveals that he would often frequent licensed premises. An entry for 14th March 1788 reads: 'Went to Friar's Oak for a bull bait to sell my dog. I selled him for one guinea on condition he was hurt but as he received no hurt I took him home again at the same price. I had all my expenses paid because I had a dog there. We had a good dinner – a round of beef boiled, a good piece roasted, a leg of mutton and ham of pork and plum pudding, plenty of wine and punch.'

The Oak was a safe house for smugglers – or rather an unsafe house on 12th February 1777 when the Horsham excise officers with six dragoons raided the premises and seized contraband worth £5,000. Their haul was sent to Horsham by four horse post chaise and later stored at the new Customs House at Shoreham.

Not surprisingly this inn, with its long and chequered history, was used by creator of Sherlock Holmes, Sir Arthur Conan Doyle as the setting for his adventure story *Rodney Stone*, the sixth impression of which was published in 1914.

It also has sporting connection – apart from 18th-century bull baiting. Licensees in the 1930s were Mr and Mrs George Jupp, parents of Vallance Jupp who played cricket for Sussex as a professional and after the war as an amateur all rounder. Today the village cricketers play on the recreation ground but still drink in the pub. The old pitch is now a baseball ground where the Burgess Hill Red Hats play.

HAYWARDS HEATH

SERGISON ARMS: Tudor brickwork lining the deep well beneath the kitchen and the massive oak front door date from the days when this was the house of a prosperous merchant. He was probably John Vynal or Vynall who died in 1599. In 1609 there is a record of the sale of a 'house, barn

and garden known as Vynalls' and it retained that name until 1832 when it became an inn known as the Dolphin. In 1845 the name was changed to the Sergison Arms, perhaps out of gratitude to the Sergison family of Cuckfield Park who presented the landlord with a fat buck each year for the traditional venison feast which was preceded by a hare hunt.

On Dolphin Fair days in the 19th century business was brisk at the inn. When a man was hired for a year he would deck his hat with ribbons and pop into the pub to celebrate. Now that job centres have replaced hiring fairs this tradition is no longer observed, nor is there an annual venison feast.

BURRELL ARMS: The first licensee, in 1871, was Ebenezer Hide who was succeeded by railway porter Frederick Ferguson who also ran a flourishing coal and coke business. He advertised 'good beds and sitting rooms' at his inn and offered his coal and coke customers reductions in price if they took a truckful. Ferguson was followed by Ernest Beeney, a local grocer, and then the licence was held by Fred 'Chubby' Tate, father of Sussex cricketer Maurice Tate who, when he retired from the summer game, ran pubs in East Sussex.

LIVERPOOL ARMS: This 19th-century railway inn may be moved if plans to extend the station go ahead. It was in July 1846 that the London and Brighton Railway Company changed its name to the London, Brighton and South Coast Railway Company and LBSCR is inscribed on the Clair Road frontage of the pub. Benjamin Goldsmark, a Cuckfield man, took over from the first licensee Richard Kennard and his daughter was the barmaid. They took in the railway company staff as lodgers and catered particularly for the engine drivers on the down line. Up line drivers went elsewhere. By 1856 the pub had become so prosperous that a visitors' handbook reported that the best rooms were 'all engaged by the visitors from London with their piles of money.'

It was in the early days of Richard Kennard's tenancy of what was then a beerhouse that there was a fatal accident on the line at Haywards Heath. A locomotive attached to the front of the Brighton bound train was derailed as it passed through the Copyhold Hill cutting. 'The bodies of the dead were taken to an adjacent public house' says a contemporary report. It was probably the Liverpool Arms.

HENFIELD

WHITE HART: When restoration work was started here in 1937 under the supervision of architect Mr A B Packham a Tudor apartment was opened up and two possibly edieval windows. Also revealed was a large fireplace with the date 1618 or 1678 – it is hard to decide whether the third numeral is a one or a seven – scratched on it. Alterations to the interior were carried out by local builder Robert Vinall whose family has been in Henfield since Tudor times.

An old well at the inn used to supply water to half the neighbourhood and in the early 1900s a cattle market was held in the garden and courtyard. It was in this courtyard that the last Venture coach to run from London ended its days. Alfred G Vanderbilt set up the service which ran every weekday to and from Brighton to London and he published its times and prices: London 10.15am, calling at Roehampton 11.15am, Old Malden 11.35am, Epsom 12.05pm, Burford 12.45pm with an hour's stop for lunch; Capel 2.25pm, Horsham 3.05pm, Red Lion, Cowfold 3.45pm, White Hart, Henfield 4.15pm, Plough, Pyecombe 4.55pm, and the Metrople, Brighton 5.30pm. Fares outside 10s., inside 15s., box seats 5s extra. On the day war broke out the Venture coach left London on time but it got no further than Henfield. The horses were commandeered for the army from the courtyard of the White Hart.

Another victim of the war was Mr Vanderbilt. He was on his

way back to America in April 1915, on the Lusitania which was torpedoed by a German submarine off Kinsale, with a huge loss of life.

GEORGE: This was also a coaching inn and it had a famous post boy called Jimmy. One day the Prince Regent's coach stopped here on its way to Brighton and the Prince, always a keen coaching man, noticed Jimmy's skill in putting on fresh horses. Holding up three half crowns in one hand and two in the other the Prince said to him: 'You can have the three if you can get to Horsham within the hour.' Jimmy did the journey with ten minutes to spare, collected his half crowns and had the Prince's patronage for ever after.

In the 1830s the George had to be sold because its owner, former Brighton coach owner Richard Pattenden, went bankrupt. After a few lean years it was business as usual and in the 1930s a celebratory dinner was held here after the centenary cricket match between Henfield and the Sussex County XI. Nelson Thomas, fielding for Henfield, went for a catch from Jack Oakes but lost sight of the ball in the sun and it hit him on the head and knocked him out.

HORSHAM

BEAR INN: Bearbaiting was a popular spectator sport in the Market Square in the 18th century and even as late as 1893 a dancing bear was displayed there. This 300 year old pub derives its name from the barbarous pastime in which, like in bull-baiting, dogs were set on to the tethered animal. At one time the carved bear above the main bar entrance had a pair of red eyes which lit up at night. It has since been replaced by an animal with more orthodox eyes, carved by a customer friend of 1960s licensee Hal Johnson.

The Bear has a strangely shaped bar. The room to the left of the front door, and the one above it are not part of the premises – they belong to the *West Sussex County Times* next door at 15 Market Street. The story goes that they were lost in a wager on a game of cards between the licensee of the Bear, perhaps Thomas Evershed who was there in the 1880s, and the newspaper proprietor, Lewis Miles.

ANCHOR INN: This pub is the former Shades section of the Anchor Hotel which had its entrance in East Street and has been converted to offices. In July, 1749 Robert Clarke, the executioner for Horsham, hanged himself with a bridle in the hayloft of the inn. He did so, it was said, because he had been entrusted with half a guinea to pay for a pig but had gambled away the money on a game of All Fours – a form of dominoes.

The Anchor's animals had a tough life. Its black cat was thrown into a mill stream with a pound weight around its neck while men wagered on whether it would get out. Fortunately it did. The pub's bull mastiff was not so lucky. It killed six lambs belonging to Horsham diarist John Baker in February 1773. 'Mr George Walker came here afterwards and said he had killed the dog which last year Mr Shelley had offered him five guineas for' he recorded in his diary.

On 18th October 1790 a most elegant dinner was served 'in the presence of the Duke of Norfolk who addressed the company in a long and animated speech on their privileges as burgesses and their rights as Englishmen.' The bill for the occasion totalled £40 4s 2d. The items on it were:

Dinners for 54 people	£6	15s.	0d.
Fish	£1	2	6
Seven dozen port wine	£9	9	0
Four dozen Lisbon	£5	12	0
18 bottles of sherry	£2	19	0
Punch	£4	12	0
Beer, porter & cyder	£2	12	6

Brandy and gin	£2	8	0
Tea and coffee		19	0
Supper for 20 people	1	0	0
Fruit	1	0	0
Bread, cheese and beer		10	0
Brokeridge		16	0
Beer for the Cryer for one year		6	8
Paper for the court		2	6

KINGS ARMS: This inn was thriving in the mid 17th century when William Shortt issued his token with the 'KING'S ARMS' on the obverse and on the reverse: 'IN HORSHAM 1667', the figure of a horse and the initials W.F.S.

For a number of years the inn was the headquarters of the Revenue men fighting the smugglers of Sussex and by 1801 it was a post office as well. Mr J Edwards in his *Companion from London to Brighthelmstone* reports that the inn has been 'much improved and modernised by its proprietor Lady Irwin' and 'here are post chaises and carriages.'

In the 1930s the Kings Arms was the meeting place of the Bungs of Horsham, a light hearted sort of charitable organisation set up for 'ye restitution of convivial nights.' Among its members it had author Jeffrey Farnol, Jimmy Walker the ex-mayor of New York City, and the Paramount Chief of the Gold Coast.

QUEENS HEAD: A young man met a violent end outside this pub in March 1830. Some of the local lads had been drinking and playing cards when they 'fell out among themselves.' The landlord, a Mr Waters, turned them out and it was then that Harry Hewett took out a knife and stabbed Edward Smith who died 15 minutes later as a result of the wound. Hewett was tried at Horsham Assizes on a charge of murder but was found guilty of manslaughter and sentenced to transportation to Bermuda for life.

'Young men! Take warning from his plight
Shun drink and cards by day and night,
Be honest, sober, kind and free,
And so avoid such misery'.

Those wise-after-the-event sentiments were expressed in a ballad sold in the streets after the trial.

The last person to be hanged at Horsham ended up in the stables of the Queens Head. John Lawrence went to the gallows in 1844, watched by a crowd of 3,000 people, for killing Brighton police chief Henry Solomon by a blow to the head with a poker. Lawrence was buried in the precincts of the prison but a year later this was pulled down and the body exhumed. For some reason, perhaps at the suggestion of the landlord, it was taken to the pub stables where it became a tourist attraction – hundreds queuing to pay twopence to view the corpse – or what was left of it.

The Queens Head was demolished in 1900, and rebuilt in 1910 at a cost of £1,000.

HOUGHTON

GEORGE AND DRAGON: A king and an elephant have stopped at this 13th century flint house for a drink. The king was Charles II fleeing to France after the defeat of his forces at the Battle of Worcester. According to the account of Colonel George Gounter (or Gunter), who was there at the time, on 14th October 1651 he left the house of his sister, Mrs Symonds in Hambledon with the king very early in the morning. He had taken the precaution of putting a couple of neats' tongues in his pocket in case he got hungry. On the way the king and the colonel were joined by Lord Wilmot and Robert Swan and they stopped for refreshment at the George and Dragon 'and still in their saddles ate the neats' tongues that the colonel had provided.'

Perhaps in the kitchens of the colonel's sister's house the neats or ox tongues had been cooked according to this 17th century recipe: 'Boil him and blanch him, cut out the meat at the butt end and mingle it with suet as much as an egg, then season it with nutmeg and sugar, dates, currants, and yolks of raw eggs, then put your meat to the tongue and bind it with a cawl of veal or mutton then roast it, basting it with butter.'

Many years later, around 1900, a circus passed through the village and the waggons stopped outside the inn. The clowns, the acrobats and the animal trainers went in for a drink but the elephant could not get through the door. Not wishing to disappoint a customer the landlord opened his first floor bedroom window and leaned out and offered the elephant a bucket of water. Pictures of the incident are on display in the bar.

Also by the large open fireplace in the Grade I listed building is a huge beech gourd which owes its splendid patina to the constant application of goose grease by an old man who used to wipe his fingers on it whenever he had had goose for his lunch.

HURSTPIERPOINT

NEW INN: In many Sussex towns and villages, in the Georgian period, Tudor timber-framed houses would be given elegant stone facades. The New Inn in the High Street certainly received this treatment but the rear of the premises still retains traces of its earlier origin.

It was here, in November 1814, that the villagers gathered to celebrate the abdication of the Emperor Napoleon with a splendid dinner. They also collected 20 guineas to distribute to the poor of the parish. Some 30 years later a Tradesman's Benefit Society was set up at the inn which then housed the weekly corn market.

In the 1920s the proprietor Alf Makins described his house on his trade card as Ye Olde New Inn with frequent bus and train services to and from Hassocks. It was, he said, 'close to the beautiful South Downs, an ideal spot' and had 'good wines and spirits.' The bus service to which he referred was operated by rival innkeeper George Boniface of the Sussex Arun Hotel who also offered waggonnettes and brakes and a special carriage with rubber tyres.

ITCHENOR

SHIP INN: The *Gentleman's Magazine* of 1803 reported that Itchenor had two public houses and a few cottages and the Duke of Richmond's house and pleasure grounds called Itchenor Park House. The Ship was one of the pubs but it was destroyed in a fire in 1934 and has been rebuilt standing back from the road in typical Henty and Constable brewery brick and timber style.

In Nelson's day they were busy building ships at Itchenor but the yards closed in the 19th century and did not open again until after the Second World War – then to cater for the needs of the yachtsmen rather than the Royal Navy. For a time the bell that called the shipwrights back to work after a lunchtime pint or three hung in the bar of the new Ship but it is there no longer. It did have some interesting regulars in the 1930s when British comedian Gordon Harker lived with his family at the Haven. His friends from the theatre who used to pop along to the Ship for a drink included Evelyn Laye and her husband Frank Lawton.

KEYMER

GREYHOUND: Until 1938 this inn did not appear under this name in the local street directories. The only entry, from 1899, was 'Frederick Neal, beer retailer'. It was, no doubt, one of the beerhouses set up under the Beer Act of 1830 whereby anyone could sell beer by paying an excise duty of two guineas. Frederick Neal died in 1938 at the age of 78, having run his beerhouse for 33 years. He was succeeded by his son Jack Neal who named the house the Greyhound.

An earlier innkeeper was Mark Taylor, a landlord with unusual sporting interests. He was a keen follower of rat matches. These were bouts between terriers and rats which were put in a pit together. Each dog would be timed as it killed the rats and the fastest would be the winner. Owners would wager heavily on the hoped-for killing speed of their pets.

KINGSFOLD

DOG AND DUCK: Not a lot of country inns can boast 10 acres of land and a regular clay pigeon shoot but this 15th-century farmhouse can. It must have been an alehouse in the 18th century because recently a Twister or spinner was removed from the ceiling of one of the bars and this device, rather like an upside down roulette wheel, was often used by smugglers to share out their spoils.

It was bought in 1906 by King and Barnes of Horsham and in those days it was still known as Little Chicken Farm. Ale and cider was sold but it was still a working farm with most of the land being used to raise stock and poultry.

Mr and Mrs Ernest Lipscombe took over the licence in the 1930s and attracted a show business clientele for the eggs they sold and the ale and the welcome they provided. Members of the Crazy Gang used to call in on their way to and from London and dates on the coast. Flanagan and Allen, whose partnership started in Florrie Forde's Flo and Co in 1924, Nervo and Knox, Naughton and Gold and Monsewer Eddie Gray were regular visitors and so was British and Empire boxing champion Len Harvey who was only too ready to challenge the locals to a game of darts.

The pub had plenty of outbuildings and the one nearest to the kitchen door was used for wedding receptions, cream teas for cyclists on their way to the coast, and, during the Second World War, as a temporary dormitory for Canadian soldiers not quite capable of returning to their units after an evening out.

Chicken stew was very much a speciality of this particular house and it was kept simmering in a cauldron over an open fire in the taproom and was occasionally stirred with the fire tongs. The locals loved their landlord. After Ernest Lipscombe died the villagers would bring the heavy barrels of ale and cider from the cellar to help his widow.

A car park was added to the premises in the 1950s, under the aegis of Mr Booker, but chickens and ducks were still ranging free around the pub. In the 1960s Mr Henry Harman obtained a full on licence for the premises and installed indoor 'ladies' and 'gents' – previously everyone had to go outside.

George Harman took over in the 1970s and the pub acquired a strong darts team, tug-of-war side, clay pigeon shoot and schoolboy motorbike scrambling. Indeed a day at the Dog and Duck is an adventure.

KIRDFORD

HALF MOON: Set in the wall of the vicarage, which is within sight of the pub, is a stone carved with the inscription:

Degradation of Drunkenness.

There is no sin that doth more deface God's image than drunkenness. It disguiseth a person and doth even unman him. Drunkenness makes him have the throat of a fish, the belly of a swine and the head of an ass. Drunkenness is the shame of nature, the extinguisher of reason, the shipwreck of chastity and the murderer of conscience. Drunkenness is hurtful to the body. The cup kills more than it cures. It causes dropsies, catarrhs, apoplexies. It fills the eyes with fire, and the legs with water, and turns the body into an hospital.

These warning words can be read by anyone leaving the Half Moon but they would have been far more visible to habituees of the Black Bear which has long since been closed. The plaque was either put up by the local temperance society, and it certainly has a 19th century temperance tone about it, or by a local vicar wishing to keep his flock on the straight and narrow. Some even say that it was the vicar that had the drink problem and this was his parishioners' way of drawing his attention to it.

The Half Moon is a Tudor style pub but has 18th-century additions by builder C T Woolridge who put his name and the date 1743 on the new facade. Still there is the old smoking cupboard in the chimney where the sides of bacon were hung to be pickled in the smoke from the fire beneath.

LANCING

SUSSEX PAD: It is a question of paying your money and taking your choice about why this inn was so called. Some say it is after the pad or raft bridge which was the way to cross the Adur in the 18th century; others that it refers to a pad or riding horse; and a third suggestion is that it refers to the thieves or footpads which once frequented the area.

Certainly an early bridge was formed of rafts fastened together and stretching half across the rimer. The ferryman would push it over with a pole when there were carriages and horses on board. And there must have been thieves in the vicinity for a society was set up to prosecute them. The *Sussex Weekly Advertiser* of 1789 announced that a meeting of the Lancing Society for the Prosecuting of Felons, Thieves and Others would meet at the house of James Carver, bearing the sign of the Sussex Pad, in the parish of Lancing on Monday, 6th July at 11 am.

A new licensee took over in 1797 and in the same newspaper, on 27th March of that year, he advertised that: 'John Matthews respectfully informs his friends and the public that he has taken, fitted up and stocked the above inn with everything necessary for public accommodation and that all favours conferred on him will be received with gratitude, and diligently attended to. Neat post chaises and good horses.'

The old Sussex Pad was destroyed by fire on 26th October 1905. The present inn is its replacement. And the present 'Spaghetti Junction' type bridge replaces the toll bridge which was built in 1781 and demolished in the 1960s.

LICKFOLD

LICKFOLD INN: The 16th-century premises that formerly occupied this site were called the Three Horseshoes and, until the main London to Midhurst road was diverted away from it in the 1830s it was a busy little coaching inn. The mail coaches called there and so did the post chaises, waggons and other horse drawn vehicles.

It was built originally possibly as a hall house as it has only one fireplace and chimney but such a large one that a fire in it heats the downstairs and upper rooms. In 1970 it came on the market and was closed for a time while it was lovingly restored with particular attention to period detail, by a former shipwright.

Now it bears the same name as the village in which, in 1332, Walter de Lickfold is recorded as the owner of Lickfold Farm. The family was still around in the 18th century when John and Edward Lickfold signed the copy of a statement in respect of a fee owing to the parish clerk.

LINDFIELD

BENT ARMS: Once known as Wichelo after an earlier owner, and then as the White Lion in Lindfield Town. Since the mid 19th century its sign has shown the arms of the family of Gibbs Francis Bent of Oat Hall, Haywards Heath, who also gave their name to Bents Wood and Bentswood Road in Haywards Heath. In 1871, when it was still Wichelo's, its assembly rooms were hired for worship by the Reverend Frederick Hamilton, minister of the Union Street church in Brighton.

When King Edward VII made an official visit to Lindfield he lunched at the Bent Arms and the landlord's wife, Mrs F J Comer, cooked for him. A later visitor was a British film star of the 1930s George Arliss, famous for his screen portrayals of such prominent people as Disraeli and Cardinal Richelieu. Members of his family still live in the area.

In 1920 the inn was badly damaged by fire and only some exceptionally brave work by fireman Fred Nye saved its roof from total destruction. When it was restored after the blaze the first floor ceilings were raised and a new attic floor added.

RED LION: The land on which this inn was built around 1790 was known as Paynes Tenement. It was leased by William Payne, John Browne and John Pelling to Thomas Dobson.

Three coaches a week passed through Lindfield and Ditchling on the way between Brighton and London. The Times, The Comet and the Age all called at the Red Lion, a name which first appeared when Thomas Grover died and his executors sold it in 1832 to Simon Mills. In 1855 the innkeeper was Simon's son, Charles Mills and he issued a brass token with the name of the Red Lion on it.

Until the first world war late shoppers would meet in the

inn yard on Saturday evenings to eat the whelks, winkles and other shellfish they could buy from the straw hatted stall-holders who used to trade there. These delicacies were always served in saucers and swimming in vinegar. Having eaten the shellfish the customer was expected to tip up the saucer and drink the vinegar.

WITCH INN: The wych elm that grew nearby gave this house its original name of the Wych Inn. When the tree was blown down the name was changed to the Bricklayers Arms. That was its name in 1868 when John Jeffrey a maltster, submitted a bill for carting flints there for road mending. Some years later the name was changed again – to the Witch – and the inn sign showed a witch on her broomstick with her cat riding pillion. A tale of the time was that there was a witch at the pub – perhaps an unpopular wife of the landlord – who would stick a pin into the footprints of a departing customer and so force him to return. Limping, perhaps?

LINDEN TREE: Not only has this inn had a name change – it has also been given a new look. When it was the Stand Up it was just that – a pub without a single seat. It was the tap for Edward Durrant's brewery, which closed in 1906, and he wanted his workers to get back to work and not loiter over their drinks. Neither did he want customers hanging around over games of dominoes or nursing a pint in a comfortable seat in the corner. 'Let 'em stand up and drink up' he would say.

Edward Durrant brewed two beers. One sold at 2d a quart and was known as apron washings or harvest beer and the other cost 8d a quart. In the inn yard there is still the old wheel which had to be turned by one plodding horse power to pump water to the brewery. The horse always wore a blindfold when at work to prevent it getting giddy.

LITTLEHAMPTON

WHITE HART: The earliest recorded date for this inn was in 1761 when it was called the Swan. Its name was changed to the Dolphin in 1772 but another Dolphin opened in the High Street in 1784 so the original Dolphin became the White Hart. Coaches on the coastal service between Brighton and Chichester and on to Portsmouth called here. They were Crosse's Earl of Arun and Stevens' Champion. They crossed the river by the Littlehampton chain ferry.

An early innkeeper was Mr Westall, stepfather of Harriet Jeffreys who had gained some local notoriety by claiming direct descent from the infamous Judge Jeffreys of the Bloody Assizes.

DOLPHIN HOTEL: Most notable visitor to this inn in the 19th century was Lord Byron who stayed here for a couple of days in 1804. Two years later, accompanied by former bare-fisted prizefighter Gentleman Jackson and a pretty young woman dressed as a boy, he sampled the hospitality of the seaside resort of Brighthelmstone.

In later years the Dolphin became a little too lively for Strict Baptist teetotaller Henry Lock. In a lecture to the Littlehampton Total Abstinence Society in 1880 he described it as the haunt of the 'break of day boys'. They were customers who would settle down in the inn's kitchen and sing 'we won't go home 'til morning'. And they kept their word.

The Dolphin was put up for sale by auction in 1882, together with its stables and two cottages. Bidding started at £1,000 but stopped at £2,850 – not far short of the reserve of £3,000.

BEACH HOTEL: In the late summer of 1778 a London solicitor, Peregrine Phillips, visited Littlehampton on his month-long tour of Sussex. His *Sentimental Diary* of his holiday was published in the same year by J Ryall of Westminster and Brighton and advertised in the *Sussex Weekly Advertiser*. Peregrine Phillips had nothing but praise for the Beach. 'Expecting to be boxed up in a little room nine foot by five foot in a small thatched cottage' he was agreeably surprised to find himself in a 'lofty, spacious parlour 24 ft by 16 ft in a handsome, large, well-built lone house called the Beach Coffee House above 100 yards from the edge of the ocean.'

Of the landlord, a Mr Jeffries, he wrote: 'A good, honest, well-tempered obliging fellow keeps this lodging house, sells a mug of ale (wish I could say good, which may certainly be said of the wine) is proprietor of two bathing machines, and works them himself; with the aid of a woman (a Mrs Zebedee) to attend to the ladies; he makes ropes; he fishes; and mends nets; goes out to sea with companies in pleasure boats; is an amphibious animal, living as much in the water as on land; in short, he seems to have as many distinct occupations as Scrub in the Stratagem.'

Phillips allusion to George Farquhar's *The Beaux' Stratagem*, first performed at Drury Lane in 1707, is not surprising. He had probably seen the play because his daughter, Mrs Crouch, was an actress in David Garrick's company and may well have appeared in it.

The Beach Coffee House was built by Peter Le Cocq in the early 1770s and became a popular meeting place for the literati and gentry who visited Littlehampton. A taproom was added to the original building in 1818 by James Tupper and in 1858 Mrs Leah Tupper was advertising the hotel for 'families and gentlemen, replete with comfort and accommodation, and wines and spirits of the finest quality.'

It was largely rebuilt in the 1890s but the remains of the original coffee house can be seen in the gardens. During the last war the hotel was used by the Royal Marine Commandos as a signals centre and lecture hall.

LODSWORTH

HALFWAY BRIDGE INN: Here, in 1760, according to the *London Evening Post*, four men ate a dog. The newspaper report of the incident states: 'On Sunday, the 11th inst, a man followed by a Newfoundland dog entered the inn where four young men were in company. One accidentally hurt the dog and the traveller complained. One of the four said 'Shut up, or we will eat your dog'. The owner said that they were quite at liberty to do so and he would give them half a guinea's worth of drink to wash it down provided they forfeited 6s each if they failed to pick the carcase clean. 'These conditions were agreed and poor Caesar was slaughtered and actually devoured by his brethren in human form.'

HOLLIST ARMS: Long, long ago – in 1425 to be precise – the manorial rolls recorded a house on this site. In 1668 an artist drew a perspective view of the property, then known as Mants House, and it is preserved in the *Cowdray Papers* in the West Sussex Record Office.

In the early 19th century Mants House had become an inn called the Poyntz Arms, after the Lord of the Manor and

Whig MP for Chichester William Poyntz. He had married Elizabeth Browne, sister of the 8th Viscount Montague, who succeeded to the Cowdray Estates on the death of her brother.

The first mention of it being called the Hollist Arms was in 1852 when it was formally leased to the Gatehouse Brewery for seven years. Colonel E O Hollist, who built Lodsworth House, inherited the pub in 1880. He planted a flowering cherry on the village green to mark the Diamond Jubilee of Queen Victoria, helped by children from the village school. 'This he enjoyed but he took no pleasure from having to attend an inquest into the death of a farm worker killed in a drunk affray outside the inn' said his great granddaughter and present owner, Mrs C H Barnes.

The family often tried to buy the green in front of the pub – and Lord Cowdray constantly refused to sell it. But the Hollist Arms does have a strip 8 feet long by 6 feet deep – to accommodate the horse-drawn brewery drays which used to deliver the beer.

Lower Beeding

CRABTREE INN: This was not the large roadside pub it is today when a party of soldiers stationed at Horsham Barracks during the Napoleonic Wars went for a walk. When they arrived at the alehouse, probably not the first one that they had called at, they demanded 'something nice to eat'. Either the landlady had nothing to hand or she did not feel like preparing a meal so she refused them. As they were about to leave they heard a canary bird singing in its cage. 'How much for the bird?' they asked. 'It's not for sale, it's a family friend' she replied. But after a little hard bargaining they persuaded her to accept half a guinea for the bird, quite expecting them to take it with them, cage and all. One of the soldiers paid her, however, while another took the bird from the cage and wrung its neck. 'Pluck and cook it' he said. This was done and the four men solemnly sat down and divided the dainty morsel between them.

Lurgashall

NOAH'S ARK: How this inn, which is nowhere near Mount Ararat, got its unusual name is not known. It has been suggested that it was because there used to be a lot of water about when a large pond existed between the church and the pub. A former licensee was called Noah Hill but he cannot be held responsible – the inn had the name for many years before he took it over.

In the 16th century when the house was built this was a

cider making area, and production was so large that the rector received 19s in cider tithes and only 5s.8d. in all other tithes. Over at Bignor the vicar did even better – he collected, in an average year, 25s.8d. in tithes on cider.

The Noah's Ark had its own malthouse, a grocer's shop and a blacksmith's forge in 1880 according to sale particulars in the Cowdray Papers. In 1956 the blacksmith's premises were sold by the brewery for 2s 6d to the village cricket club – on condition that the club did not sell beer there.

MIDHURST

SPREADEAGLE: 'The oldest and most revered of all the prime inns of the world' wrote Hilaire Belloc of the Spreadeagle in his *This and That of Inns*. It was originally a Tudor hunting lodge and Queen Elizabeth I may well have stayed here when she was sumptuously entertained in 1591 by Sir Anthony Browne, first Lord Montague of Cowdray. That was quite a party. For breakfast on Sunday morning the company consumed three oxen and 140 geese, then followed a couple of days of hunting and more feastings and on the Wednesday the lake at Cowdray was dragged and the net emptied at her feet. An account of the 'Honourable Entertainment given to the Queenes Majestie in Progresse in Cowdrey in Sussex by the Right Honourable the Lord Montacute' was published the same year.

Many years later workmen discovered the inscription 'the Queen's Room' on some panelling which had been covered with white paint – a convenient confirmation of the royal visit.

It was to Sir Anthony Browne that Mr Hollist wrote 'from the Eagle Inn' asking for his support for a Bill in Parliament to make the river Wey navigable from Guildford to Godalming. Another transport problem was dealt with at meetings in the

Spreadeagle in 1740 and 1749. It was decided to raise a mortgage of £400 secured on the tolls, to repair the road from Hindhead. A year later the Duchess of Richmond agreed to lend £400 at 4 per cent, secured on the tolls of the Hindhead to Chichester Road.

Deeds in the Cowdray Papers credit the Spreadeagle with a multiplicity of owners but this was a device to get a vote at Parliamentary elections. In one instance the freehold of the inn was granted to a yeoman of Graffham and to a yeoman of Woolavington on the same day.

Today the Spreadeagle is a three star hotel. And until a few years ago a uniformed flunkey was on duty outside the main entrance to look after guests as they arrived.

ANGEL HOTEL: In the garden of this ancient inn is the remains of a wall dating from around the time of the Norman Conquest and a lead pump from around 1666, the year of the Great Fire of London.

Some early visitors were a group of emigrants on their way to Southampton where the *Mayflower* was waiting to take them to the New World. The Pilgrim Fathers, for that is who they were, always called inns that received them kindly Angel Inns. This piece of Anglo American history is depicted in a mural in the hotel's restaurant. It was painted in 1970 by Ronald Fraser, an illustrator of the *Radio Times.*

The inn was expanded to cope with the coaches when they came rolling along and extensive yards and stabling constructed to cope with the increasing traffic on the Dorking to Chichester road. By 1882 the railway was the latest thing in transport and the Angel's proprietor John Parker proudly advertised that he was the appointed agent of the South Western Railway Company.

Part of the Hotel was at one time the Angel Steam Brewery which supplied beers to five pubs in Midhurst. The local petty sessions were held there, in what is now the residents' lounge, and the court cabinet, where the clerk and the usher would keep their robes, is still in place.

Also preserved in the grounds is Midhurst's first bowling

green. It now has a preservation order on it and is not used for play.

NEWBRIDGE

LIMEBURNERS ARMS: A Charles II shilling was found under the floor of the bar of this inn near Billingshurst when it was being dug out in the 1960s to give more headroom under the oak beams. Perhaps it was dropped by a former occupant of one of the three thatched cottages that now form the premises. The shilling was on show in the bar but some years ago it was stolen. The present inn dates from the turn of the century. The original Limeburners Arms was half a mile away – down by the wharf and canal basin where the Arun Navigation meets the Wey and Arun Canal. These

waterways were at their busiest in the early years of the 19th century. In 1805 lime kilns were built to burn the chalk brought up river from the coast and limeburners lived in the cottages that were converted to the present inn.

In the canalside storehouse at Newbridge, ledgers were found which contained the names or numbers of the barges that used the waterways and details of their cargo. When the railway came in the 1850s the freight and the passenger traffic fell off and the canal traffic dwindled away to nothing in the 1880s.

Newpound Common

BAT AND BALL: Around the time the first games of cricket were played on the common, with a curved bat and a single stump, the front of this 16th-century farmhouse was extended and this inn opened for business.

It was in 1910 that William Trayton Stanbridge, father of the present licensee, acquired the tenancy of a beerhouse, shop and six acres of land from brewers G S Henty and Sons of Arundel. He installed a bakery oven and ran the shop as a grocery and drapery business, his customers having no objection to trying on frocks among the fruit. In 1926 the pub was acquired by Horsham brewers King and Barnes in an exchange of premises deal. They also acquired the Stanbridges. Ted Stanbridge was two years old when his father came to the Bat and Ball and he has lived there for the past 76 years.

During the war there were some 1,300 French Canadians and a regiment of Royal Engineers stationed at Rowner, near Billingshurst, and they used to patronise the pub and stay there until the beer ran out. One evening Ted and his father served the thirsty soldiery with three full barrels (36 gallons) of beer. It was not until 1952 that the Bat and Ball beer only licence was changed to a full on licence.

In front of the pub, where the summer game used to be played, is a large pond which Ted Stanbridge has stocked with more that 1,000 goldfish. He has to keep watch for visiting herons – customers he does not encourage for the sake of his fish.

NORTHCHAPEL

HALF MOON: One of the greatest cricket all-rounders – and a speedy runner – was Noah Mann, licensee of this 14th century inn from 1756. Every Tuesday he would run the 20 miles to Hambledon to practise with members of that famous club. John Nyren, writing in *Cricketers of My Time* in 1833 described Noah as 'a fine batter, a fine field and the swiftest runner I ever remember'. This left-handed bowler and batsman was also a skilful horseman and his party trick was retrieving from the saddle, at full gallop, handkerchiefs that had been thrown on the ground.

Noah Mann died suddenly and tragically at the age of 33. He had been out for a day's shooting and returned home soaked to the skin. Still in his wet clothes he drank with friends late into the night and then sat down in front of the fire and went to sleep. In the night he collapsed onto the embers and died from his burns. The fireplace into which he fell is still there.

Another celebrated licensee of the Half Moon was Mrs Wilkinson, mother of Thomas Wilkinson who took over the Lamb at Angmering in 1850 and held its licence continuously for 57 years. But he did not beat his mother's record – Mrs Wilkinson was at her inn for 61 years.

OVING

THE GRIBBLE: A gribble is a small marine borer which eats its way into the wood of the waterline of boats and is a general nuisance to mariners. But this thatched inn in a rural backwater south of the A27 has a brewery which produces Gribble Ale, Red's Tipple, Pig's Ear and Black Adder and has no connection at all with the marine isopod.

It is called after Miss Rose Gribble for whom, in the end, the course of true love did run smooth. For years she lived alone in the thatched cottage from which the inn was later converted, pining for her lover who was married to another. What made the affair so poignant was that the wife of the man she loved was mad. Years passed with everyone growing older – until one day the wife died and Colonel Hussey and Rose Gribble were free to marry and live happily ever after. ...

That was a long time ago. The Gribble Inn opened in 1980 and started its own brewery in 1987. Licensee Paul Tanser bought the Bosham Brewery, a one man business run by Philip Turnbull, who had decided to turn to horticulture on a full time basis. The Pig's Ear brew is so called because it turned out stronger than intended and not at all according to the recipe. Black Adder is a winter ale with a definite festive feeling.

Among the customers who turn up regularly at the Gribble for the home brews is TV astronomer Patrick Moore, who lives not far away at Selsey, and singing superstar Petula Clarke who has a daughter at school in the area.

PETWORTH

ANGEL HOTEL: These premises started out in the early 16th century as an open hall house to which a chimney was added about 100 years later. In John Taylor's 1636 survey of the taverns of Sussex the town of Midhurst is credited with four and the innkeepers were named as John Kelsey, Anne Carus, Mary Hudson and Joan White. There is the usual preponderance of women for they used to brew the ale and serve it while their menfolk toiled in the fields. No doubt the Angel was one of the taverns but it does not appear as such in any documents until February 1691 when Robert Trew was recorded as having 9,000 poles of hops worth £18 on the 7 acres of the Angel's hop ground.

Thomas Hampton was the landlord in 1720 when he bought from George Trew, presumably Robert's son, the malthouse and stables on the other side of the road. He was the sitting tenant. In the Land Tax return of 1753 the Angel is assessed at £4 and in the Window Tax Assessment of 1762 Thomas Hampton was recorded as having 13 windows. The minimum rate of tax was 3s and this was imposed on houses with up to seven windows. After that it rose fairly steeply. An eight window householder had to pay 11s., a nine windower 12s., and after that it went up by about 1s.6d. a window. Mr Hampton therefore had to pay 13s.6d.

A number of inventories relating to Petworth inns and alehouses have survived and they show that most of them held a good stock. For instance John Goodman in 1619 had four hogsheads and a barrel full of beer valued at £4 or 4d a gallon and he had containers for a further 600 gallons. He also had a quantity of wine, including sack, claret, white and sweet wine, worth a total of £33.

RED LION: This inn was originally called the Little White Hart – but only after another Little white Hart in Trump Alley had closed down. And that Little white Hart had its diminutive prefix to distinguish it from the White Hart, which was indeed a splendid place. Surviving inventories from 1670 and 1758 show that it had 24 rooms and outbuildings and 11 of the rooms were painted and four of them had names: Griffin, Hart, Marigold and Angel – no doubt as a result of their decoration.

Henry Mitchell bought the Little White Hart in New Street in 1752 and his daughter Mrs Langley inherited it in 1775. In 1792 it was sold to Arundel brewer Edward Puttock who changed its name to the Red Lion. He also bought the Bull and changed its name to the Star.

POYNINGS

DEVIL'S DYKE: This pub, 700 feet above sea level, was totally destroyed by fire in 1945 and rebuilt in its present form in 1954.

The first inn on top of the Downs, only a stone's throw from an Iron Age hill fort, was a wooden hut which used to stand on wheels at the top of Ship Street in Brighton in 1818. It was, according to a newspaper account 'well stocked with a profusion of refreshments' and its landlord was a noted fiddler Tommy King. In 1831 a small inn was built to replace the hut and this was gradually extended to become a luxury hotel and a major attraction in the Brighton area. It was visited by many important people, among them William IV, Queen Victoria accompanied by Prince Albert, Gilbert White of Selborne and Rudyard Kipling.

James Henry Hubbard, a Brighton hotelier, bought the Devil's Dyke estate in 1892 and built up its attractions until he had 30,000 visitors on Whit Monday in 1893. There was everything for everybody. The hotel had a coffee lounge large enough to accommodate 275 people and its walls were hung with valuable oil paintings. A tea house in the grounds, called the Bungalow, could accommodate 200, and the amusements included shooting galleries, swings and roundabouts, test-your-strength machines and a bicycle railway. The Dyke Park Estate Brass and Reed Band would give concerts at weekends.

A railway was built from Hove to the Dyke in 1887 but passengers had to climb the further 200 feet to the hotel on foot. The line flourished until the 1920s as it was a particular favourite with golfers, but in 1938 it closed for good. James Hubbard gave his backing to a cable railway scheme which operated between 1897 and 1908 and also backed a steep grade railway on the north side of the hill. However, in 1907 he had to emigrate rather rapidly to Toronto – for financial reasons.

The hotel's heyday was around the turn of the century. When the motor car took over from the train numbers of visitors fell away and later licensees were always looking for gimmicks to attract more trade. In the 1930s, when television started from Crystal Palace, the Devil's Dyke was the ideal place to receive the signal. It was not 700 feet above sea level for nothing. Licensee Fred Piggott installed an eight inch television set and people flocked out from Brighton to look at it.

In the 1970s lessees of the rebuilt hotel, gift shop proprietors Mr and Mrs Kramer, had the bright idea of putting a model of the Egyptian temple of Abu Simbel in the newly constructed car park. They intended to transport tons of sand to the site and have replicas of the 70ft high statues of Rameses II dotted about – to commemorate the Egyptian government's fine archaeological efforts to save the originals from flooding from the Nile by moving them piecemeal to higher ground.

But the Department of the Environment did not like the idea. The nearby Iron Age hill fort was scheduled as an Ancient Monument and the department felt that one was enough in the area.

PULBOROUGH

SWAN INN: The old Swan was demolished in 1958 and the new one built further back to allow the road to be widened. It had been a busy coaching inn, accommodating the top paying customers while the coachmen and servants were put up at the Running Horse across the road.

One market day farmer Jackie Dallyn rode in from Hardham on his pony and had a drink or two too many at the Swan. At closing time his friends put him on his pony, but facing the animal's tail rather than its head. The pony made its own way home and at a wayside pond near Hardham Green decided to have a drink itself. Farmer Dallyn slid off gently into the water.

The new Swan was flooded in 1968 and it took weeks to dry out and a lot of stock and business was lost. Locals blamed the new high banks beside the Arun for the flooding. They had been constructed to keep the southern fields of the Amberley Wild Brooks free of water so they could be cultivated.

RED LION: In this 400-year-old inn, when it was 300 years old, the landlady was killed in her own skittles alley. On 26th June 1776 the *Sussex Weekly Advertiser* reported: 'The mistress was crossing her ninepin alley where some men were at play when she was unhappily struck by a bowl on her temple, which was going at great force. It fractured her skull in a most shocking manner. She was soon after trepanned but to no good effect as she languished to Saturday and died in the greatest agony. The verdict of the inquest was accidental death.'

PYECOMBE

PLOUGH INN: On 7th February 1849 the body of Brighton brewer George Stonehouse Griffith was found by some men out shooting between Dale Gate and the Plough Inn. He had been shot and his pockets rifled. His whip and a cut rein found nearby suggested that he had been the victim of an attack by highwaymen. An inquest held at the inn returned a verdict of wilful murder against persons unknown. Rewards were offered for information leading to the apprehension of the killers but they were never traced.

The mystery of this murder started a month earlier. A letter addressed to 'Mr Mertens, Griffis Bruery, Brighton' was received by the head clerk of the Rock Brewery, Mr Martin. 'Some parties intend to rob you next time you goes to Horsham, so bee on your guard' it stated.

In view of this threat Mr Griffiths, proprietor of the brewery, decided to go to Horsham himself on 6th February. He hired a gig and armed himself with two pistols. On his return journey he stopped at an inn in Henfield and told the landlady that one of his weapons was loaded, the other unloaded. He passed through Terry's Cross tollgate at 9.05pm on the bright moonlit night but never reached the next toll at Dale Gate, where the tollkeeper was expecting him. Several witnesses said at the inquest that they had heard the sound of a shot at about 9.30pm – presumably the one fired by the murderer or murderers. Beside Mr Griffiths body was found the unloaded pistol, which had been pulled. In his pocket was the loaded one.

Seven years later a gold watch belonging to George Griffith and part of its chain was found when a pond at Newtimber was being cleaned out.

RUDGWICK

KINGS HEAD: The churchyard of the 14th-century church of Holy Trinity runs down to the back door of this inn but the vicar, the Rev T A B Charles has no problems with tankards among the tombstones, most of which have been moved anyway. There has, however, been conflict between pub and pulpit in the past. In the 1950s they nearly had recourse to law to settle a dispute about frontages and the prospect of litigation prompted people to dig into the deeds. These revealed that the Manor of Goring in 1742 granted a 999 year lease on a property described as 'ye hovel'.

Ye hovel developed into a busy coaching inn, frequently patronised by the Prince Regent on his way between Windsor and Brighton. This royal visitor and his entourage brought prosperity to the village and perhaps this sudden affluence inspired a local rhymster to write:

Rudgwick for riches
Bucks Green for poors
Billingshurst for pretty girls
Horsham for ......

The post-war increase in the popularity of the motor car caused problems for both pub and church. Where were their patrons to park? Eventually a strip of land on the opposite side of the road was acquired for a car park for the pub which has been happy to share it with the parishioners of Holy Trinity on high days and holy days.

RUSPER

PLOUGH INN: This 15th-century house was once a hospice run by an order of nuns who would dispense food, drink and shelter to passing pilgrims. The ruins of the mother house, or nunnery, were demolished in 1781 and replaced by a Georgian house named the Nunnery.

Also in the 18th century – in 1793 to be exact – a hog was killed here which stood 12 hands (four feet) high, measured 9ft 6ins from the nose to the tip of the tail, and weighed 116 stone 6lbs – only a little lighter than the 117 stone 2lb monster killed at the Three Crowns in Wisborough Green in the same year.

RUSTINGTON

LAMB INN: The turn of the century was pub rebuilding time in Rustington. The Lamb, built in 1832, was replaced by the present building in 1902 and provided with a large hall on the site of the cobbler's shop which was part of the previous premises. This hall was often hired for smoking concerts from which women were strictly excluded, and it was also where the Rustington Silver Band, later amalgamated with the Littlehampton Silver Band, gave its concerts. Part of the hall was used for less entertaining purposes – it was the local mortuary.

WINDMILL INN: A new inn was built on the site of the old one in 1908. Although the premises changed, the landlord remained the same – Henry Ralph Booker. But when the little thatched tea huts were built in the gardens Henry set up as a confectioner and pastrycook as well as selling beer. In 1935 a Mr C Booker, presumably Henry's son, was advertising in the Littlehampton Visitors' Guide that he was the proprietor of the Tea and Pleasure Gardens of the Windmill Inn and he was also a baker and confectioner and a manufacturer of 'Home Made Bread, White Meal, French and Milk Bread. Teas could be provided for any number at the shortest notice. Fruit and Flowers. Swings and Croquet. Established 60 years.'

The Windmill after which the earlier pub was called was Humphrey's Mill, a smock mill brought to the site in the 1850s either from Station Road, Angmering or from the bottom of Sea Lane where there were two mills. It was pulled down in 1910 but the miller's cottage still remains.

SELSEY

NEPTUNE: When it was called the New Inn, around the turn of the century, champion boxers were trained in the gym at the back of this pub. Among them was Bombardier Billy Wells who was never beaten on points, although he was knocked out twice by Georges Carpentier – once in the fourth round at Ghent and again a year later in the first round of a bout at the National Sporting Club. Wells was the first heavyweight to win the Lonsdale belt outright but he lost his title to Joe Beckett in 1919. Even to people not interested in boxing Billy Wells became a familiar figure for he was the man who smote the gong for Rank Films.

Licensee James Northeast was a keen sportsman and it was his enthusiasm and that of farmer Sidney James Wiggonton of Grange Farm, where Billy Wells lived while training, that established the inn as a boxing centre. Other champions who sparred in its gym were Pat O'Keefe, who won the first British middleweight title in 1906 and then again 12 years later; Billy Bannon; Bermondsey flyweight Sid Smith who outpointed Joe Wilson over 20 rounds to win the first Lonsdale belt at this weight; and Stoker Smith. The boxers entered into the life of the village when they were not in strict pre-fight training. Once Billy Wells competed in a swimming race in the Selsey regatta and was beaten easily by fisherman Bert Pennicord. 'Come on, you can take me on at my sport now' said the defeated champion as they walked out of the water. Bert wisely did not accept the invitation.

LIFEBOAT: Until it was modernised and extended about 20 years ago this was the Albion, a beerhouse patronised by local fishermen. It came as a bit of a surprise to the village policeman Peter Ogden to be asked by a carload of Americans one day in the early 1960s: 'Say, where do we go to find the pirates and the smugglers that live around here. ... is it the Albion?' He directed them to the pub but could not convince them that it would not be full of chaps with wooden legs, eye patches, striped jerseys and with parrots on their shoulders.

SHERMANBURY

BULL INN: When the present inn was built in 1893 the earlier alehouse at Mockbridge was converted into two cottages. They were demolished in the 1970s, much to the fury of the people who wanted them preserved. The bull-dozers moved in and down came the cottages to become the pub's car park – just the day before a preservation order was put on them.

The inn is not called after the farm animal or a papal edict but after a Cowfold family called Bull who were yeomen in the 16th century and then spread around Sussex, one branch coming to Shermanbury. A Simeon Bull moved to London in 1750 and his great grandson William Bull became MP for Hammersmith, president of the Royal Albert Hall and, in 1922, Maltravers Herald Extraordinary.

SHOREHAM

RED LION: A highway robbery and its macabre conclusion; a woman soldier who received an allowance of half a guinea a week from George IV and died aged 108; and the glass covered coffin of a burglar – all passed through the doors of this 16th-century tavern for which the annual rental used to be 4d.

The highway robber was heard boasting of his crime by Phoebe Hessell who at the age of 15 had fallen in love with a soldier called Samuel Golding and disguised herself as a man and enlisted in the Fifth Regiment of Foot so she could go to the West Indies with him. Later she and Samuel were posted to Gibraltar where he was injured and invalided home. Phoebe revealed the secret of her sex to the commanding General and was quickly and quietly discharged from the army. The couple were married back in England and lived together happily for 20 years until Samuel died. After a short widowhood Phoebe married William Hessell who died in 1792. By then she had become something of a character and local friends gave her a donkey on which she carried fish for sale around the neighbouring villages. She was on a fish selling expedition when she dropped into the Red Lion for a drink and heard 24-year-old James Rook boasting that he and

Edward Howell had robbed a man carrying the mails of half a sovereign at Goldstone Bottom. Phoebe passed this information on to Constable Bartholomew Roberts and Rook and Howell were arrested, tried and convicted. They were hanged publicly at the site of the robbery on 26th April 1793, and their bodies hung in iron frames on the gibbet until they decayed.

While the bodies were decomposing James Rook's old mother would steal out of her cottage in Old Shoreham every night and pick up the pieces that had fallen to the ground. She put the remains in a chest and buried them devoutly in the churchyard.

History does not reveal if Phoebe Hessell attended the execution of the young robber. However, it is recorded that she attended the coronation of George IV, sharing a carriage with the vicar of Brighton, and that the king called her a 'jolly old fellow'.

The man under glass at the inn was another robber who had broken into Buckingham House in the 1850s and had been shot by a manservant while trying to escape. The body was exhibited at the Red Lion in a coffin with a glass lid in the hope that someone could identify the felon. It was the burglar's faithful dog that gave his master away – it would not leave the coffin of John O'Hara who, like James Rook, was buried eventually in Old Shoreham churchyard.

A convivial New Year ceremony took place at the Red Lion until the time of the First World War. It was called the 'Bushel' which, according to the *Sussex Daily News* of 5th January 1883 involved the decorating of a bucket with green paper and flowers and filling it to the brim with ale 'so the froth loomed over the greenery like a cauliflower'. The ale was ladled into pint glasses by a baler and served free to all comers.

SWISS COTTAGE: There were amusements of all kinds in the pleasure gardens set up by James Britton Bailey, a local ship builder, in 1838. The Swiss Gardens became the mecca for day trippers when the railways came to Brighton and the visitors enjoyed to the full the theatre, the archery, the bowls, the boating and the refreshment room which could accommodate 1,000 people. There was a magic cave, frequent firework displays, and the occasional hot air balloon ascent. By 1844 Mr Bailey's theatre had been licensed for dramatic performances, vaudeville and farces.

During Mr Edward Goodchild's ownership the pleasure gardens were still an important feature in the social life of Shoreham but as the years passed rougher elements moved in and their popularity declined. Much of the area was later occupied by the local council school and the Swiss Cottage of today is but a shadow of its former self. But there is still some of the ornamental lake left and still some reminders of leisurely Edwardian afternoons – even if it is only the ducks.

SIDLESHAM

CROWN AND ANCHOR: Parts of this inn are said to date from the time of the Domesday Book when the Manor of Sidlesham was held by the Bishop of Chichester, from which it was leased by list, or copyhold. In 1607 the Manor was sold and the new lords were Adrian Houghton and John Thompson of West Stoke who granted the farm, as it then was, to a tenant for 8d a year. The house came into the hands of John Middes of Midhurst in 1721 and he was the first tenant to be described as a victualler. His sister, Mary, was in need of cash so she mortgaged the Anchor to a Chichester maltster called Henry Curtis and a few years later, in 1762, sold the premises to him outright. Curtis quickly sold them on to Mary Wooldridge and the next change of ownership was not until 1821 when Bognor brewer William Hardwick bought the inn.

In the manorial lease the tenant had the right to graze his sheep and cattle on the common land and wastes of the Manor of Sidlesham. In 1763 the commons were enclosed and the right of pasture was sold off.

Evidence of Roman occupation of this part of Sussex was found when Victorian archaeologists, digging in the Anchor grounds, discovered Roman coins, spearheads and other implements.

SLINDON

NEWBURGH ARMS: There has been an inn in this village since 1716 but it was converted to the post office when the Newburgh Arms was built in the mid 19th century.

The licensee from 1871 was an ebullient character called Frank Fleet. He was an almost too generous host, plying the men carting flints for the new village school with tankards of hot gin on Boxing Day. They got so drunk that they could not unharness the horses. And in 1884 the foreman was encouraged to drink so much beer when building the infants' school extension that he cemented his tankard into the wall. It is there to this day.

One New Year's Eve Frank Fleet, his son George, and a sheep shearer called Tom Bateman were so full of ale that they rang the church bells in the middle of the night and then staggered to Mr Lane's house, took his waggon out of the shed and pushed it along Dyers Lane, down Church Hill and into the pond. The angry owner rushed out in his underwear and threatened the miscreants with the police if they did not get the waggon out and return it to his house.

The Arms has always been the centre of village life at Slindon. It is still the headquarters of the cricket club, and once inquests were held there. In 1864 the coroner had to inquire into the death of Jack Peachey who was found dead beneath an overturned cart after the horse he was driving bolted and jumped over a hedge.

SOUTH HARTING

WHITE HART: Harting Old Club, a friendly society dating without a break from 1812, holds its annual club feast at this inn on Whit Mondays. The quarterly subscription to the Old Club is 4 shillings which entitled members to a weekly payment of 10s when they were ill or unable to work. There is an elaborate system of fines for any breach of the society's rules.

On the feast day the pub is decorated with beech leaves and members meet there in the morning wearing red, white and blue rosettes and carrying hazel wands that have been peeled for a length of two feet, leaving only six inches of unpeeled bark for a handle. The procession forms up, lead by two stewards carrying their wooden staves of office, followed by two standard bearers with the club flags which have three horizontal red, white and blue stripes (as in the national colours of the Netherlands), the band and then the members with their wands. They all march widdershins around a beech bough set up in the centre of the square and then process to the church for divine service. Then it is time for the feast. ...

How this little local ceremony with its wands, beech boughs and other quaint customs came about is not known. It is something that built up over the years until now it is hallowed by tradition and attracts the crowds.

STAPLEFIELD

VICTORY INN: This pub on the village green was formerly a grocer's shop but the owner decided to turn part of it into a bar parlour selling the beers of the Southdown and East Grinstead brewery which had its headquarters in Lewes. It was taken over by Tamplins in 1923.

Grocer Charles Ede's first application for a licence was refused by the justices so he waited for a while and then applied again, this time successfully. 'What shall I call the pub?' he asked a director of the brewery as they walked out of court. 'We've just had a victory, why not call it that?' was the reply.

JOLLY TANNERS: The London to Brighton pair horse coaches used to stop here and George IV, when Prince of Wales, was a frequent visitor.

The stop for lunch at Staplefield was quite a feature of the journey. The coaches drew up under the famous black cherry trees and the passengers would pick the fruit, if the birds had not been there first, and partake of the rabbit pies which were a particular delicacy of the house. These lunchtime stops always lasted at least two hours.

Henry Michell bought the Jolly Tanners for his West Street, Horsham brewery in 1837 for £400. 'I was offered £50 more for it before I left the saleroom', he wrote in his diary. 'It proved a great bargain as it always yielded five per cent interest besides a good beer trade. ...' In 1869 he spent £100 on repairs to the premises.

STEYNING

WHITE HORSE: The present pub is not the White Horse mentioned by Harrison Ainsworth in *Ovingdean Grange*. After a fire in 1949 those premises were turned into the post office and a butcher's shop. In 1614 they belonged to William Holland, one time mayor of Chichester, who endowed Steyning Grammar School and also laid a charge of £5 on the inn to aid the older poor of the parish. William Holland's name is carved into a beam of the Royal Arms at Chichester so he probably owned both inns – but perhaps at different times.

An 18th century VIP who spent the night at the White Hart was Charles James Fox, great statesman, great gambler and boon companion of the Prince of Wales. News of his presence quickly got around and the church bells were rung to welcome him. 'Every demonstration of respect was shown him and next day the constable and burgesses waited upon him with an address' reported the *Sussex Weekly Advertiser* on 15th August 1796.

In 1806, when the barracks at Steyning were full of soldiers preparing to embark to do battle with Bonaparte, a wing was added to the inn and its upper room used as an officer's mess. After Waterloo the local magistrates court was held in that room until Parliament ruled that courts must not be held on licensed premises because witnesses tended to become intoxicated.

CHEQUERS: This building dates from the early 15th century and it was an inn in 1580 when John Stamen, a sidesman, told the bishop that on the Sunday before St James' Day he left the church during evening prayer 'to see good rule according to my oath' and found innkeeper James Holland, a churchwarden, Richard Pellett and John Kok drinking in service time.

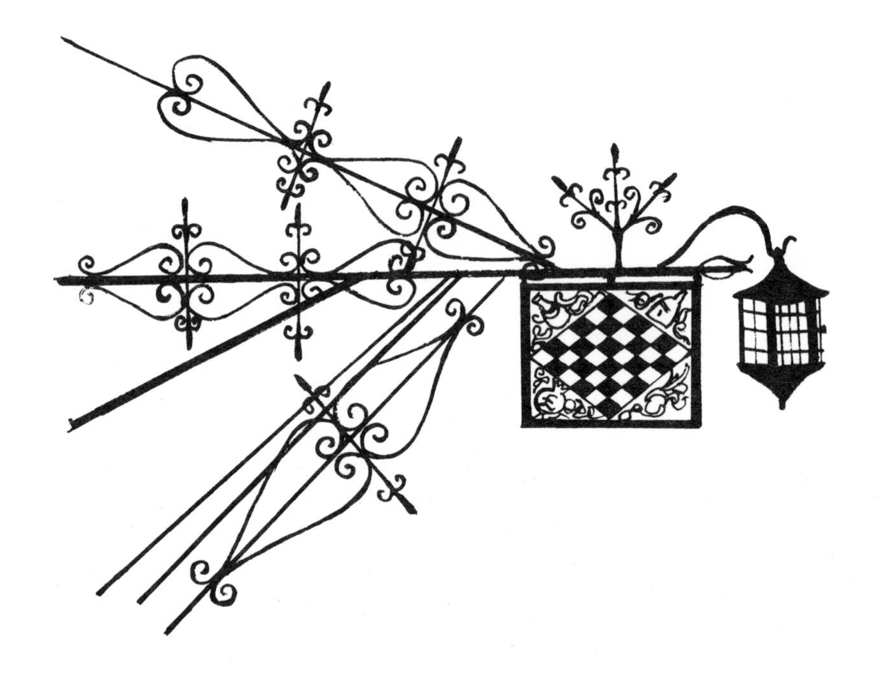

Some years later, in 1664, at another bishop's visitation John Kidder was reported for 'entertaining youths to tipple in his house at the time of Divine Service'.

The chessboard style inn sign was, in the inn's earlier days, an indication to the traders in the nearby market that the house had a chequered cloth or board which could help them with their financial calculations. This obsolete method of accounting has gone into the language as 'exchequer' and 'cheque'.

From the wrought iron bracket on which the sign was mounted hung the town lantern. In the 18th century, when it was lit at nightfall, travellers pass ng through Steyning were required to spend the night at the borough house, opposite the Chequers, rather than travel in the dark unprotected.

The river Adur is nearby at Upper Beeding so it is not surprising that the Adur River Commissioners held their annual meetings at the Chequers.

Stopham Bridge

WHITE HART: In the Napoleonic Wars men in the various county militias were encouraged to transfer to line regiments by the offer of a bounty of £7 10s per man. Some 500 volunteers from the Royal Lancashire Militia made their way to Sussex but at Chichester they were told they would have to get themselves to Horsham barracks before they could get their bounty money.

On 23rd August 1807 a party of these militiamen set out for Horsham. They stopped at Stopham Bridge for a drink but the landlord of the White Hart did not serve them as quickly as they would have liked. They turned him out of the pub and helped themselves to his stock. They ate and drank everything they could find and then smashed the place up.

News of the riot reached the constable at Pulborough and he got a posse together and, armed with picks and forks the men of Sussex set out for the White Hart. A pitched battle took place in which both locals and Lancastrians were injured, some rather badly.

In 1939 when on a walking tour with his wife Mr Eric Holden, now of Steyning, stayed at the inn for bed and breakfast. 'We were each charged 3s 6d and had to take candles to light us to bed as there was no electric light' he recalls. 'We were there again in 1948, this time bed and breakfast was 7s 6d each and there was electric light. That pub, like so many in country districts in those days, could not provide a full living. The landlord worked as a bricklayer and drove a hire car and his wife ran the bar during the day.'

STORRINGTON

WHITE HORSE INN: There was an inn on this site in Tudor times, reputedly containing timbers from broken up Spanish galleons after the defeat of the Armada. The building was extended in the 1880s but the work was done so badly that the whole lot collapsed into the street soon after it was completed.

Before the collapse it had been a busy coaching inn and when the railway came to Sussex the landlord, Mr Lee, saw its trade potential. In 1861 he announced that he would run an omnibus – horse drawn, of course – from Storrington to Worthing on Mondays, Thursdays and Saturdays to deliver passengers to the station to catch the 10.48am train to Brighton. The return journey would start on the arrival of the 5.20pm from Brighton.

A White Horse landlord with sporting tastes was Ernest Hammond, captain of the village cricket team that played a match on ice on Chantry Mill pond on 7th January 1891. Each player was wearing a top hat. The match started at 2pm and Hammond's XI won by nine runs.

His son was proprietor of the inn in 1939 when Sir Arnold Bax, Master of the King's Musick, arrived for the weekend with a couple of suitcases and stayed until he died there 11 years later.

TANGMERE

BADER ARMS: When Douglas Bader, Johnnie Johnson and other Battle of Britain air aces were flying from Tangmere this pub had not been built. The fighter pilots used to frequent the upstairs bar of the Unicorn in Chichester. The landlord, Arthur King, was a good friend to them and his bar was full of their autographed photographs. The Unicorn closed in 1963 and the Bader Arms opened in 1981 to provide rest and refreshment for the occupants of the 500 to 600 houses that are to be built in the area during the 1980s. Group Captain Bader was at the opening and was slightly critical of the portrait of him on the inn sign.

TINSLEY GREEN

GREYHOUND: Marbles have been played here between Ash Wednesday and Good Friday for the past 300 years. But beware – if the game goes on past noon on Good Friday your marbles are confiscated and stamped into the ground.

It all started, according to local legend, in the reign of Good Queen Bess. Two gallants were competing for the favours of a fair young maid and they vied with each other at archery, falconry and wrestling. The result of each match was a draw. That only left marbles for as there is an odd number there has to be a winner.

The game is played in a big ring – concrete circles with an inner ring of eight foot in diameter. It became a competitive sport under the British Marbles Board of Control in 1926 but it started as a children's game in ancient Egypt and was brought to Britain by the Romans in the first century AD. One of the early champions was Sam Spooner who notched up his first win in 1892 and used the same marbles to win again in 1937.

It was in 1932 that Eric Harman, a chiropodist from Horley, dropped into the Greyhound for a drink, and was introduced to the sport of marbles by the locals. He was so impressed by their skill that he gave a silver cup for competition in memory of his wife. Then the brewery came up with the offer of a barrel of beer for the runners up – which is why at marbles the best team always comes second.

During the war there were no marbles matches but they were revived in 1946 and the competitors included George Prentice, the ex-Scottish schoolboy champion; Sam Bailey, the Durham Wizard; and Big Bert Botting of the Southern Railway. It was necessary to have 300 clay marbles to hold the championships and before the war most of them came from Japan, packed in cartons and labelled TINSLEY GREEN MARBLES.

To play the game 49 marbles are placed in the pitch and each competitor takes it in turn to try and knock them out. Shooting must be by thumb only – a wrist movement is called a fudge and the shot is disqualified.

WASHINGTON

FRANKLAND ARMS: It was Hilaire Belloc who put this pub on the map by writing so fulsomely about it in *The Four Just Men*.

The extract reads: 'Caedwalla, King of Sussex, sent to the Pope 20,000 barrels of ale. . . . He conquered all Sussex and all Kent and was mighty before his 80th year and all on the ale of

Washington – Michell's ale of the Washington inn. Of such potency it was!'

Henry Michell was a Horsham brewer and he also had premises at Steyning, and at Brighton. His brewery was taken over by the Rock Brewery in 1911 and this eventually went to Whitbread.

The pub which Belloc credited with producing the 'Cervissian nectar' was named in honour of William Frankland of Muntham Court, Findon, who died in 1805 or his nephew Henry Cromwell, who took the name of Frankland and was later known as Admiral Frankland. Uncle William was an inventor, scientist, collector and engineer. Nephew Henry was promoted Vice Admiral of the Red in 1810. He started in flag rank as Rear Admiral of the Blue in 1801.

West Chiltington

QUEENS HEAD: According to a 'Traveller's Companion' of 1637, now in the British Museum, Charles Johnson was the tavern keeper here. Later the rector's grandson ran the pub. The original Queens Head was demolished at the end of the 18th century and replaced by the present building which has one of the earliest Sun Insurance Company's lead plaques on its wall. It is still a regular meeting place for many of the village organisations, and full of photographs of the village in Victorian times.

West Hoathly

CAT INN: A murderer with blood on his hands turned up here for a drink one night in 1734. Jacob Harris, a pedlar, had previously called at the Royal Oak near Ditchling and, while his horse was being groomed, drawn a knife and slit the landlord's throat. He then attacked a serving wench, murdered the landlord's wife and made off with what valuables he could carry. He was drinking calmly at the Cat when he heard that the militia men were after him. He rode away to Selsfield House where his friend Thomas Stoner offered him refuge. But the riding officers pursued him and while they were drying their uniforms in front of the fire they heard the sound of coughing. Harris was hiding in the chimney.

He was captured and tried and convicted of murder at Horsham. No reason was given for him killing three people. He had often lodged at the Royal Oak and was well known to

Miles, his wife and the maid Dorrity – all three of whom are buried in Wivelsfield churchyard.

The oak panelling round the bar at this inn is from the fermenting vats of a brewery in Lewes.

WEST WITTERING

THE OLD HOUSE AT HOME: This old ale house acquired the full on licence of the Dog and Duck in 1920 when that inn was converted to a restaurant and later was turned into a private house.

The Old House was originally a thatched cottage serving ale to the few farmers and fishermen who lived in the area. As the local population was augmented by more and more summer visitors it expanded and when the Schneider Trophy air races started in 1929 business became even brisker and the pub was enlarged even more. Across the road from it lived Sir Henry Royce, the engineering side of the Rolls Royce partnership, and it was in his studio in sight of the Old House that he designed the Merlin engine which was to power the Spitfires that helped to win the Battle of Britain.

WISBOROUGH GREEN

THREE CROWNS: In 1793, when Mr Older was the landlord, a large hog was killed at this inn. The *Sussex Weekly Advertiser* of 18th February reported that it measured 8ft 6ins from nose to tail, and in girth was 7ft 6ins and in height 11 hands, 2ins. Its weight was 117 stone 2lbs. 'At the current rate of 3s 3d per stone the value of the hog was upwards of £19' continues the report. 'Judges felt that if it had been fatter it would have weighed 150 stone but it had pined and refused food from the loss of another hog. ...'

WORTHING

ANCHOR INN: Tramps passing through Worthing were in the habit of dossing down in the courtyard of this inn for the night as it was conveniently situated between the coast and London roads. Parish records dated 27th February 1830 rule that any vagrant remaining at the Anchor or other lodging house more than one night and then falling ill should be supported by the landlord of that house. This regulation encouraged innkeepers to keep their courtyards free of dossers but they were not always successful. The records state that on 2nd April 1831 Catherine Butcher applied for pay for nursing a woman confined at the Anchor. She did not get the money and the Beadle, James Bassett, was ordered to see the woman out of town. On 31st March 1847 Ellen Smith, a vagrant at the Anchor, had two children lying dead. She was given 2s 6d by the Guardians for their coffins.

The Anchor is the only one of the five pre-1830 Beer Act inns to survive in Worthing. It originally had a garden in the front surrounded by a wall with some steps let into it for mounting horses. The inn sign was an anchor hanging from an upright pole and it was then known as the Golden Anchor. George Marley, the landlord who died in 1825 was succeeded by George White who opened the garden onto the road so that the inn could be seen from North Street. The land at the rear of the inn, when it was not occupied by tramps, was used by travelling circuses and for displays of horsemanship.

George White went on to become the first manager of Worthing Gas Works in 1833.

WHEATSHEAF: A rather shamefaced John Levett took over the licence of this inn in 1839. He had just lost his job as Worthing's Town Crier because his voice was not considered strong enough – and him an ex-sergeant major of the King's Dragoon Guards who had served at Waterloo!

John Levett ran the Wheatsheaf for just over 10 years. He died in February 1850 at the age of 69, and was buried in Broadwater. The pub retains its slight civic connections for it is near the town hall, courts, library and other council offices.

JOHN SELDEN: Until 1915, when the licensee was Mrs Elizabeth Schooley, this one-time beerhouse was called the Spotted Cow and it served the villagers of Salvington.

As the area was developed with the expansion of Worthing the name was changed to commemorate a famous son of Sussex, John Selden, who was born in a house nearby called Lacies in 1584. Selden was a writer, scholar, lawyer and statesman – and a good friend of Ben Jonson. He was a member of the Third Parliament which, before it was dissolved by James I in 1622, revived the right of impeachment. For this, and for other things the King did not like, he and John Pym were thrown into the Tower. Charles I offered John Selden the office of Lord Keeper of the Great Seal but he politely declined it. His autobiography, written in Latin in his own hand, was bought in 1898 for 1s and now reposes in the Bodleian Library, Oxford. Of himself Selden says: 'He enjoyed the friendship of every rank, and was frequently favoured with that of the best, the most learned, and the most illustrious. Nor was he without very unfriendly censures of impudent mouths, which he bore with manly dignity. He was frequently elected a Member of Parliament both when there was a King and when there was none.'

YAPTON

SHOULDER OF MUTTON AND CUCUMBERS: This 200-year-old inn has not only a strange name but a strange history as well. Part of it was once used as the village mortuary and at the inn, in 1898, a thatcher sold his wife to a ratcatcher for 7s 6d. – and a quart of beer.

The name, which was in the Guinness Book of Records in the 1960s until it was overtaken by a pub in London which had been given an even longer name, refers to an old Sussex recipe for mutton. William Verrall, who succeeded his father Richard as master of the White Hart in Lewes, gives details of it in the cookery book he published in 1759. The mutton is roasted in the usual way and to make the sauce William Verrall says: 'Cut your cucumbers into quarters, fry them in butter, then stew them in a little stock with chopped parsley and lemon juice'.

There is an apocryphal story doing the rounds that gives another reason for the inn's odd name. It is said that a parcel was left behind by a departed guest and when the soggy, bloodstained package was opened it revealed an uncooked shoulder of mutton and a quantity of cucumbers. ...

The last recorded incident of the old Sussex custom of wife-selling was in 1898 when a Yapton thatcher by the name of Marley sold his spouse to ratcatcher Seeby White, who was lodging at the Shoulder when the transaction took place. The new couple lived happily ever after.

Lookout on the former Ship Inn, Worthing

Appendix I

Inn Signs

Inns have always indicated their presence with a sign of some sort. A bunch of vine leaves hanging outside a house was the Roman way of saying that there was wine for sale within and this tradition continued in England long after the Romans left.

Alehouses used a long pole called an alestake to announce a new brew. A couple of such stakes appear in the Bayeux Tapestry – on the house next to one that had been set on fire. If the alehouse was also a tavern and had wine for sale as well, the stake would be embellished with a bush of evergreen or ivy leaves.

After 1267 when the Assize of Bread and Ale was introduced to regulate the price and quality of a brew, the alestake was also a method of summoning the ale-conner or ale-taster. This local government official's job was to test the ale before it was sold and this he did by taste, sight and smell. He did not, unless he was exceptionally eccentric, pour some ale onto a wooden bench and then sit on it motionless for half an hour or so to see if it would stick his leather breeches to the planking. In one version of this story if the breeches stuck the ale was of top quality – in the other version the reverse was the case.

As ale houses increased in numbers their owners looked for ways of distinguishing one from another – there not being a lot one can do to make an alestake look interesting. They started to hang carved symbols on their stakes, of such familiar things as the sun, the moon, stars, or the heads of farm animals. Soon the houses became known by the name of their signs – the Sun, Half Moon, Seven Stars, Bull, Ram etc. This early form of folk art was encouraged by Richard II who in 1393 ordered brewers to hang out a sign when they had ale for sale – or forfeit the brew.

And hang out signs they did. By the 17th century many signs had become wonders as innkeepers vied with each other in outdoor advertising. Largest of the lot was the extravaganza outside the White Hart at Scole in Norfolk which cost more than £1,000 in 1655. It arched right across the road and its supporting pillars were covered with carvings of mythological figures. There was Jonah emerging from the whale's mouth, Diana about to shoot an arrow at Acteon, Neptune on a dolphin's back and Charon carrying a witch off to Hades. Hanging from the centre of the sign was an almost life-size carving of a white hart.

Signs of this sort obstructed the roads they crossed and many of them were banned by an Act of Parliament of 1797. But one has survived in position to this day in West Sussex. It is outside the George Hotel, a frequent port of call for the Prince Regent and his entourage in the coaching days, and stretches across the High Street of Crawley which used to carry the main London to Brighton Road before the bypass was built. It has been restored and altered frequently in the passing years to ease the passage of high sided vehicles but St George on his horse still does battle with a ferocious dragon in the centre of the transverse beam.

The more modest and orthodox inn signs – painted boards swinging from cast or wrought iron brackets – have changed little in the past 500 years or so. There are the religious ones like the Three Crowns at Wisborough Green, which symbolises the three kings who brought gifts to the Christ child, and there are hundreds of heraldic signs. Among the most popular is the White Hart, the badge of Richard II, and the Red Lion from the badge of John of Gaunt. Distinguished local families have their coats-of-arms featured on many signs. The Pelham buckle and the Shelley shells occur in both West and East Sussex and there are quite a few Dorset Arms. But some, such as the Newburgh Arms at Slindon and the Hollist Arms at Lodsworth, relate to the Lordship of the particular manor to which the inn once paid its rents.

Innkeepers have always reflected the interests of their patrons which accounts for the prevalence of such sporting signs relating to the chase such as the Hare and Hounds, the

Fox, the Stag, the Dog and Duck and those relating to the games people play such as the Cricketers, the Bat and Ball. They also reflected the occupations of their regulars and there is often a Bricklayers Arms near a brickworks, a Two Sawyers in woodland, a Limeburners in chalk country, a Shepherd and Dog in the Downs.

The most popular of all inn signs is the Crown. Other reflections of royalty are Kings Heads and Queens Heads, featuring monarchs of various periods in history. The Kings Head at Albourne is a bit of a shock, however, as it features King Kong. Charles II's route when he fled through Sussex to the coast after his defeat at the Battle of Worcester produced a rash of Royal Oaks after the Restoration but few can rightly claim the fleeing king called there. He definitely stopped at the George and Dragon at Houghton – which is still called the George and Dragon.

Fashions in inn signs come and go. And the signs themselves have a limited life as they are exposed constantly to wind and weather. Outside the Crown and Anchor in Shoreham is a 9-foot tall pirate with a crown in his left hand and an anchor at his feet. He stands on the prow of a ship which protrudes above the pavement. This splendid figurehead was made for the inn in the 1930s by Mr F J McGinnity of Brighton who carved it from a solid block of teak he had recovered from a ship salvage yard at Woolwich. The whole effigy weighs three quarters of a ton. It replaced a previous figure of a sailor of the days of Nelson, also carrying a crown and with an anchor.

Another of Mr McGinnity's signs covers the whole frontage of the Ship Inn in Worthing which has been carved to represent the stern of a 17th-century ship of the line with the figure of a sailor on lookout in the crow's nest on the mast. The Ship closed some years ago and the premises are now the offices of a building society but Worthing Borough Council has ruled that the frontage must stay as it is.

The Kings Head, Bolney

Appendix I

INN GAMES

Darts and dominoes, quoits and cribbage, shove ha'penny and snooker, bowls and billiards – nowadays petanque and pool – all are games played in pubs or outside them.

In the past the sports were crueller. The average pub patron of the 17th–19th centuries saw nothing odd or cruel in cock fighting, bear and badger baiting, even clergymen indulged in throwing at cocks at Eastertide. As many of them spent their working lives in hunting, shooting or fishing to feed their families, the death of a bird or an animal meant nothing to them if it was done in the way of sport.

It was not until the 19th century that legislation banned the bull and badger baits and the cock fights that had been so popular with the patrons of the inns of Sussex. A few cockpits remain – there is one at Goodwood – and some bulls got away with it, as at Hove in 1810 when the baited animal broke its rope and charged the crowd.

Indoor games, however, have had a much harder time. Various governments have legislated against games of chance and often the issue of a licence for an alehouse depended on conditions forbidding the playing of dice, dominoes, assorted card games and skittles 'at the time of divine service'.

The Puritans were particularly punitive. Not only did they legislate against the playing of games, they forbade maypole dancing and horse racing as well.

The traditional pub games of Sussex have survived in spite of everything. There are plenty of places where they still play ring the bull, devil among the tailors, toad-in-the-hole. At Hastings they even play loggetts, a game banned in the 17th century.

Darts is, of course, the most popular of all pub games. It became a national craze between the wars and now there are some 6 to 7 million regular players. It may have originated as a knife throwing or indoor archery contest using the end of a beer cask as the target.

Dominoes probably originated in China but was introduced to England by the French prisoners of war in the 18th century. It was because he lost at a version of the game called All Fours that Robert Clarke, the Horsham public executioner, hanged himself in the hayloft of the Anchor Inn in 1749. What really worried him was that the money he lost had been entrusted to him to buy a pig.

Shove ha'penny, or shove penny as it is often called in Sussex because the metal discs are larger, dates from Tudor times. It is played on a wooden board divided into sections with strips of brass. The object is to get a total of three discs into each 'bed' or strip.

Snooker, billiards and bar billiards, as well as the later arrival, pool, can be found in town pubs which have the space for a separate games room. These games also turn up in the resort towns and holiday villages where often the pub is also the local entertainment centre like the Ship at Winchelsea Beach.

Marbles, of course, means the Greyhound at Tinsley Green, where the British Individual Marbles Championships are held every Good Friday. But the game is also played at Battle on Good Friday – before 12 noon of course. Anyone playing marbles after that time would have them confiscated and stamped into the ground.

Two games or pastimes that crop up in occasional pubs in East and West Sussex are toad-in-the-hole and ringing the bull.

Toad-in-the-hole requires the competitors to throw heavy metal discs into a hole in the centre of a lead cushion mounted on a low table with a drawer in it. Competitors stand 8 feet away from the target and score two points for every disc that goes into the hole, one point for each one that remains on the cushion, and nothing for the ones that fall to the ground. The object is to score 31 points and this score must be achieved exactly – you bust if you score 32 and must try again for the exact number.

Ringing the bull has its variations throughout Sussex. In

some pubs, such as the Blackboys Inn at Blackboys, the 'bull' is a stag's head, in others it can be just a hook on the wall or a complete bull's head or perhaps just the horns. A metal ring hangs from a line attached to the ceiling and the object of the exercise is to swing it across the room so it lands on the target. In the Swan at Lewes in the 1930s there was a regular customer who would stand with his back to the bull and ring the hook in its nose every time.

Devil among the tailors is a form of table skittles which originated in the 18th century. It is not often met with today. Real skittles, the outdoor sort, are played at the Black Horse in Findon, and at the Wilkes Head at Eastergate they have introduced the game so popular with the French, boule.

Funny fund raising games such as dwile flonking (allegedly invented by the students of Leeds University in a rag week in the 1960s), wellie throwing, piano bashing, china breaking, all have their place in the social scene but cannot be taken too seriously. Video and quiz games also come and go ... but darts goes on for ever.

Bibliography

Ancient Arundel. Mervyn D Francis.
Arundel Castle Archives.
Brighton Herald.
Catalogue of the *Cowdray Archives.*
Catalogue of *Wiston Archives.*
CAMRA's Real Ale and *Real Pubs in Sussex,* 1987.
Chichester Observer.
Chichester Papers edited by Francis Steer. Chichester City Council.
Chronicle of Edburton and Fulking. F A Howe. Hubners Ltd.
Glimpses of Old Worthing. Edward Snewin.
A History of Harting. Rev H D Gordon.
History of Pagham. Lindsay Fleming.
Metropolis of Mid Sussex. Wyn K Forde and A C Gabe. Charles Clarke (Haywards Heath) Ltd.
Mid Sussex Through the Ages and *The Story of Burgess Hill.* Albert H Gregory. Charles Clarke (Haywards Heath) Ltd.
A Millenium of Facts in the History of Horsham and Sussex. William Albery.
Mid Sussex Times.
Reminiscences of Horsham. Henry Burstow (1911).
Reminiscences of Littlehampton. Eva Robinson and J S Heward.
Sussex County Magazine. 1929–1956.
Sussex Daily News.
Sussex Archeological Collections.
Sussex Weekly Advertiser.
West Sussex Gazette.
West Sussex County Times.
Wakehurst Place, Sussex. Gerald W E Elder.
Worthing Road and its Coaches. Henfrey Smail.